# THREE TALKS

KAPNICK FOUNDATION DISTINGUISHED
WRITER-IN-RESIDENCE LECTURES FOR 2021

# THREE TALKS

Metaphor and Metonymy
Meaning and Mystery
Magic and Morality

BRENDA HILLMAN

University of Virginia Press
CHARLOTTESVILLE AND LONDON

The University of Virginia Press is situated on the traditional lands of the Mona-can Nation, and the Commonwealth of Virginia was and is home to many other Indigenous people. We pay our respect to all of them, past and present. We also honor the enslaved African and African American people who built the University of Virginia, and we recognize their descendants. We commit to fostering voices from these communities through our publications and to deepening our collective understanding of their histories and contributions.

University of Virginia Press
© 2024 by the Rector and Visitors of the University of Virginia
All rights reserved
Printed in the United States of America on acid-free paper

*First published 2024*

9 8 7 6 5 4 3 2 1

LIBRARY OF CONGRESS CATALOGING-IN-PUBLICATION DATA

Names: Hillman, Brenda, author.
Title: Three talks : metaphor and metonymy, meaning and mystery, magic and morality / Brenda Hillman.
Description: Charlottesville : University of Virginia Press, 2024. |
Series: Kapnick Foundation distinguished writer-in-residence lectures
Identifiers: LCCN 2024013654 (print) | LCCN 2024013655 (ebook) | ISBN 9780813949437 (hardcover) | ISBN 9780813949444 (ebook)
Subjects: LCSH: Poetics. | Poetry—History and criticism. | BISAC: LANGUAGE ARTS & DISCIPLINES / Writing / Poetry | POETRY / Subjects & Themes / Political & Protest | LCGFT: Lectures.
Classification: LCC PN1064 .H55 2024 (print) | LCC PN1064 (ebook) | DDC 808.1—dc23/eng/20240507
LC record available at https://lccn.loc.gov/2024013654
LC ebook record available at https://lccn.loc.gov/2024013655

*Cover art and design:* Joel W. Coggins

This book is dedicated, with immense gratitude, to Edward B. Germain (1937–2024) and to Charles Wright, two of my early teachers, and to my students over nearly four decades, from whom I have learned so much.

# CONTENTS

# FOREWORD

I want to begin this foreword in 1997, during the early days of the internet, long before Big Tech began mining our data and we willingly had our heads in the Cloud. Amazon was a mere two years old, only just toddling toward world dominance, and poetry entered one's life not through algorithms but through the more sidereal patterns of chance. Poetry books were so unevenly distributed then, and outside of urban centers or research libraries, small and university press titles were especially hard to access. A disquiet at the fringes of mall chain bookstore orthodoxy like fragments of Gnostic gospels, such books, when the knowledge they carried did enter one's life, could do so *entirely* unanticipated, upending everything forever without warning.

Which is what happened when the editor of the literary journal I worked for asked if I wanted to review *Loose Sugar*, a new book by the poet Brenda Hillman. I was a first-year MFA student, and Hillman was unknown to me. "Sure," I said. Though I was learning from peers and teachers who deepened my understanding of contemporary poetry, I was also already frustrated with the period style. The late-nineties post-confessional poem: its left-justified one- to two-page block of lines narrated in first person was already widely mocked as "the workshop poem." Dissatisfied with form, dissatisfied with content, I intuited a wider range of formal and aesthetic possibilities than I had at hand. I sensed an amplitude inside poetic language I couldn't yet access myself, and I was actively searching for poets who knew the way.

In Hillman, I lucked upon such a poet. In reading *Loose Sugar*, I unwittingly enrolled in a very different kind of writing program, one taught by a visionary whose poems were unlike any I'd encountered. A guide who gently instructed me to read differently, who gradually expanded my concept of poetic literacy, Hillman reintroduced me to *mystery* in its root sense: to be initiated into knowledge. And her poems brought me nearer to its Greek root, μυέω, a word that once indicated the closed eyes or mouth of the initiate. "Read this by your own light, / little body," croons one tender lyric in the book, "read this with your eyes closed." I dimly sensed such light in myself, and though I was thrilled by this encounter with paradox, I knew I didn't yet practice an inner literacy through which I might access the power to illuminate the word.

I never wrote that review, of course! At the time, I found that many of the poems in *Loose Sugar* hovered just beyond the edge of rational comprehension. Nonetheless, their resistance to conventional logic felt familiar, a skewed take on the wisdom literature of my religious upbringing. And though I couldn't review the book, I couldn't stop returning to it either. Its mysteries were invitations: to come closer to both knowing *and* unknowing, to engage with irresolvable questions about the nature of time, spirit, matter, morality, love, and suffering. And now, after decades of reading Hillman's work, I know that finding *Loose Sugar* difficult at first simply meant I'd never before read a book of contemporary poems that asked me to read it, eyes closed, by the light of my own inner light.

I'd also probably never read a book of poetry by a West Coast poet other than Robert Hass (Hillman's husband), who bridged what was then a stark cultural divide between the "establishment" East and antiestablishment West Coast poetry cultures. Then, as now, the poetry taught in most creative writing programs leaned distinctly toward the establishment East. That was another reason *Loose Sugar* seemed charged with the power of Gnostic heresy: the work came out of the San Francisco Bay Area's "vibrant experimental women's writing community," as Hillman describes it here, "inspired somewhat by Objectivist writing, Black Mountain, and San Francisco Renaissance writers, but approaching these traditions through women's experience." In stark contrast to my graduate program, in the Bay Area, "the possibilities for poetry exploded to include more process, 'nonpoetic' materials, non sequitur, and polyphonic voices, inventions in formatting, hybrid genres, and subject matter." When I moved to the Bay not too many years later, I'd find and embrace those same possibilities. *Loose Sugar* prepared me to do so.

Like life itself, Hillman's poems play out on multiple planes simultaneously, a vivid mix of metaphysics, intellect, autobiography, eros, politics, and aesthetics. The poems of *Loose Sugar* acknowledge that we get divorced and raise kids among questions of time and eternity, we fall in love and have sex as material and spiritual and political beings, we fight crippling personal depression while governments wage forever wars whose bloated budgets increase economic inequality, and the formal life of poems can encompass achieved, finished wisdom as well as the messier and more incomplete processes of not-knowing and of maybe-coming-to-know. A young poet, I'd been enrolled in a workshop-based education of prescriptions and proscriptions, of death by a thousand platitudes: write what you know, tell the truth but tell it slant, find your voice, find your line, etcetera. Reading Hillman's work tilted all the tired truisms; it encouraged me to write into unknowns, to seek truth without expectations, to explore my many voices, and to remain flexible about my craft.

After I moved to the Bay, I was not surprised to learn that Hillman is a beloved teacher of and canny advocate for poetry. A longtime professor at Saint Mary's College and core faculty of both the Napa Valley Writer's Conference and the Community of Writers, she has as an educator long stood for what she calls "permission to be strange, to bring together in your reading and writing what you encounter in your inner world." These three Kapnick lectures, dedicated to two of her early teachers and her many students, offer ample evidence of her ability to encourage and permit not just formal risk but also rangy capacious language, unorthodox metaphysics, and direct political action. They also give us access to the fundamental ideas, beliefs, and practices from which her mature poetry has sprung. Since

*White Dress* first appeared to acclaim in 1985, she has published ten more celebrated books, her dual career as poet and pedagogue an exemplary lesson in teaching from a place of eternal apprenticeship to and exploration of one's own artistic, spiritual, and political lives.

Consistently inventive and adept at adapting to change, Hillman has written poems equal to our lives and equally responsive to the times in which we live. She is, above all, a seeker, perhaps more at home in the search than in certainties. As she writes in "Metaphor and Metonymy," the first of her lectures:

For about six decades of writing poetry, I've wrestled with the same questions over and over. Some are ontological: Why does the universe exist? How does the spirit world fit with ordinary matter? What is the inaccessible meaning of nature and existence? Some questions are aesthetic: What is poetic language? How much strangeness am I permitted as I represent my experience in poetry? How can I best represent, to quote Marianne Moore, "an imaginary garden with real toads"? Some questions are autobiographical: Who was I in my childhood? What is my subjectivity beyond being a white grandmother-poet-teacher with an unruly inner life? What is a Brenda anyway? And some of the questions are social: Who is my audience? What is

a human among species? What are the moral, polit-
ical, and scientific responsibilities of poets? Live the
questions, writes Rilke.

This book is the result of a long, productive life as one of
our most vital poets, one who has, from the very start,
lived the questions with unwavering commitment.
Though her essentially lyric practice relies on the figu-
rative language much poetry relies on, its unusual am-
bition encompasses both the moral vision of anti-war
and environmental activism as well as the mysteries of
an active, nonconformist spiritual life. The summa of a
life's work, these three lectures offer us a full, lucid, and
accessible articulation of a complex, sui generis poetic
practice. To read them is to enroll in a School of Ques-
tions whose curriculum encourages and empowers
each of us to pursue our own lines of inquiry.

Hillman has pitched these lectures as a poetry
toolkit, an approach that allows her to model how to
read and write poems from a place of openness and
curiosity, without what Keats would call "irritable
reaching after fact and reason." The lectures build on
each other and in increments fully realize a practice
of reading across many modes of poetry. Instead of a
prescription for "correct" interpretation, instead of per-
forming close reading as a decoding of a poem's one

true meaning, Hillman reads instead by close *noticing,* practicing critical description with unerring, sometimes uncanny sympathy. Reading alongside her can be genuinely revelatory, transformational especially when she describes poems we think we already know; her descriptions of Stevens, Dickinson, Duncan, Eliot, and Jarrell are particularly peak experiences. Hillman's close noticing works in tandem with personal narrative, mini-lectures, and minifestoes to create a self-portrait of the poet at work, and at work in the world. Taken together, these lectures also act as a wisdom book that inspires both by example and by exhortation to go out and do good.

As she documents in her third lecture, "Magic and Morality," going out and doing good is an integral part of Hillman's mature poetics. In the decades since I first encountered her work, she has completed a now-iconic ecopoetic quartet of books on the classical elements: *Cascadia, Pieces of Air in the Epic, Practical Water,* and *Seasonal Works with Letters on Fire.* With *Practical Water,* Hillman instigated her reportorial practice of drafting poems during activist actions, often with the aid of trance. These remarkable documents have become part of a much larger body of what she calls "crypto-animist activism" which, as she writes here, is "the practice of communicating with or being aware of nonhuman objects, creatures, or presences during . . . direct actions." One of her recent books, *Extra Hidden Life, among the Days,* gathers together all the modes of writing in her elemental quartet, its short neo-Symbolist lyrics, reportorial poems, journal poems, elegies, and odes plunging us into the present day while also theorizing the relationship between art and life, lyric and political action, human and more-than-human lives.

Expanding her formal and thematic range considerably, her ecopoems and crypto-animist activism articulate a bioregional consciousness rooted in Northern California, its geological formations, watersheds, and unique species. They also develop further her pointed anti-war, anti-capitalist, and feminist critiques, and innovate a method of documenting activism and political coalition through poetic reportage—all while also continuing Hillman's lifelong project of remaining true to the shape of one woman's life through lyrics of musical immediacy, formal ingenuity, and memorable phrasing. "There are so many types of / 'personal' in poetry," she writes in "String Theory Sutra," a poem from *Pieces of Air in the Epic.* "The 'I' is a needle some find useful, though / the thread of course is shadow . . . a twin existence." Like the thought-worlds of certain Gnostics she has admired, hers is a nondualist dualism, a split vision whole unto itself.

Hillman's work has long insisted on the primacy of paradox to experience, preserving being's essential, expansive strangeness. In her ecopoems and crypto-animist activism, she's turned this vision into the locus of a capacious moral imagination that draws readers into relation with what can't always be seen of this "twin existence" but *can* be known, if only intuitively. "An ethics occurs at the edge / of what we know," she writes in *Practical Water*'s title poem. "The creek goes underground about here." At the edge of the unknown, attuned to the underground, Hillman locates the fierce, difficult beauty of the ontological and political situation we share with all matter on this planet. It's from insisting that "Everything feels everything" and "There are no spaces between us" who are all citizens "of matter and beyond" that Hillman's mature work gathers moral authority. "The poet reaches more deeply into the human order not to center it but to get past the ego," she writes in "Magic and Morality," "to a place where the language and the earth touch and meld with the noticing."

By now it should be obvious that I never graduated from the School of Questions, in part because Hillman's never stopped schooling me in poetry's possibilities. Since 1997, I've anticipated the release of each of her books as I've anticipated new books by few other living poets: each has been a curriculum of its own, offering masterclasses in the formal imagination, the moral life of environmental writing, and the political dimensions of the lyric. Few contemporary poets have had such ambitions for their work, and few have pushed their art so far into the unknowns that connect us and all life on Earth. Hillman's work reveals to its readers wisdom as necessary, omnipresent, and as overlooked as the lichen to which she dedicates one recent sequence of poems. "The job of a soul is to stay awake," she writes there, and in reading these lectures, I'm reminded that wakefulness in its largest sense—open mind and open heart alert to odd beauty, mystery, and justice—is what I've learned and continue to learn from Brenda Hillman's work. And I'm grateful that, with the publication of these Kapnick Lectures, we're all able to go to school with her.

BRIAN TEARE
CHARLOTTESVILLE, MAY 2022

# PREFATORY NOTE

These talks were delivered while I served as Kapnick Writer-in-Residence at the University of Virginia in Spring 2021. Because of the pandemic, they were delivered online to an audience of writers, students, and the general public, each one about forty-five minutes, followed by a moderated question and answer session.

I decided to keep them more or less as they were delivered, though I've added a sentence or two here and there. The example poems are referenced sometimes briefly and sometimes in a bit more depth, so the reader will find here a bouquet of considerations, some presented mainly for a quick appreciation. It's to be hoped that the compact format will create enjoyment for the student, the specialist, or for the general reader.

# THREE TALKS

# METAPHOR
*and*
# METONYMY

IT'S SPRING 2020 as I begin to work on my talks for you. COVID-19 lockdown is in full force. Now it's January 2021 as I revise this paragraph. I've been following the path of white moths, or maybe cabbage butterflies, fluttering over the kale in our garden, riddled with powdery mildew.

Cabbage white butterfly

They seem multidirectional like the world-soul as described by Hegel. Deliveries are being made by people emerging from ominous windowless trucks to set bags on the porch. I'm aware my husband and I have multiple advantages; we can afford to have food delivered, we work from a home we own; we are white. We have disadvantages too; we are elders in a society that throws away older people, even older poets. The virus dangles its thread of RNA like a tilde on a vowel in Portuguese. *Adenine cytosine guanine uracil.* In the strange quiet of the first weeks, the minuscule strands leap from human faces less as avatars of death than as searchers and yearners, trying to make proteins.

|   |   )   |   |   \   |   |   |   |   \   |   |   |   \   |

I'm honored to be invited by faculty, staff, and students at the University of Virginia to serve as the Kapnick Writer-in-Residence for 2021. Hearing about the tradition of the public talks, I conceived of three interlocking talks that would be a toolkit for your daily lives as writers and as readers. I had thought I would be in Virginia, but instead, I'm imagining you, my audience of listeners and readers, in your little squares all over the country. I've come to think of Zoom as a kind of quilt of imagined universes.

I hope to speak to you in these three talks in a jargon-free way about things that have energized my practice of being a poet and a human being. Being human still seems like a practice. I've thought all year about the nearly impossible task of sustaining the imagination right now. My three talks will address six forces of poetry. Tonight, Metaphor and Metonymy; next week, Meaning and Mystery. In two weeks, Magic and Morality. I want to negotiate across perceived differences in these pairings in hopes of giving you the energy that poetry can bring as we live through a series of profound historical crises together. I hope something I say will help your life.

|   |   |   |   |   |   \   |   |   |   |   |   \   |   )   \   |

For about six decades of writing poetry, I've wrestled with the same questions over and over. Some are ontological: Why does the universe exist? How does the spirit world fit with ordinary matter? What is the inaccessible meaning of nature and existence? Some questions are aesthetic: What is poetic language? How much strangeness am I permitted as I represent my experience in poetry? How can I best represent, to quote Marianne Moore, "an imaginary garden with real toads"? Some questions are autobiographical: Who was I in my childhood? What is my subjectivity beyond being a white grandmother-poet-teacher with an unruly inner life? What is a Brenda anyway? And some of the questions are social: Who is my audience? What is a human among species? What are the moral, political, and scientific responsibilities of poets? Live the questions, writes Rilke.

| | | | \ | | | | \ | | | ) \ |

To begin, I'd like to share a poem by Yannis Ritsos, the great Greek poet whose work many American readers know via the translations by Edmund (Mike) Keeley.

### Miniature

The woman stood up in front of the table. Her sad hands
begin to cut thin slices of lemon for tea
like yellow wheels for a very small carriage
made for a child's fairy tale. The young officer sitting opposite
is buried in the old armchair. He doesn't look at her.
He lights up his cigarette. His hand holding the match trembles,
throwing light on his tender chin and the teacup's handle. The
    clock
holds its heartbeat for a moment. Something has been
    postponed.
The moment has gone. It's too late now. Let's drink our tea.

Is it possible, then, for death to come in that kind of carriage?
To pass by and go away? And only this carriage to remain,
with its little yellow wheels of lemon
parked for so many years on a side street with unlit lamps,
and then a small song, a little mist, and then nothing?

This piece demonstrates powerful moments of metaphor imbedded in an apparently realist narrative poem. Here is an isolated moment between two people—a woman and a young male officer; the implication is that they are would-be lovers, but it is nowhere stated. We know that he is nervous ("His hand holding the match trembles") and that whatever was going to happen will not happen. "The clock holds its heartbeat" is a great type of metaphor—personification. The figures are isolated, the setting is interior, and the carriage of desire and/or death is outside—here, an imaginary vehicle with wheels made of lemon slices. The English version switches from past tense to present tense. The lemon slices are at first devices of realism; then, with a single stroke, they become metaphoric wheels that take the moment somewhere else. As the woman is making the soldier's tea, the sense of loss is amplified by the dailiness of ritual and choice. With another line, "Is it possible, then, for death to come in that kind of carriage?" the poet further pushes the lemon wheels as carriers of death. The poem, of course, is by now itself a carriage. There is little consolation as the last lines seek to make an accommodation between the image of the carriage, almost fairytalelike, and a profound adult disappointment. The coach, with "its little yellow wheels of lemon / parked for so many years on a side street," is a deft vehicle for what the characters barely realize; they somehow could have climbed out of having tea into another life had it not been for an unacknowledged fate or infinite delay. It's mysterious the way the little lemon slices so elegantly create emotional power. Though this poem enacts a narrative of lost opportunity, the metaphor permits a sense of strange and tragic delight.

| | | | \ | | | \ | | | | ) \ |

In our garden, a Steller's Jay stages its appeal outside. There are many subspecies; it is loud, annoying, and mostly not vegetarian. Because of its pointy black crown and hood, this bird always reminds me of an executioner of Robespierre in 1789. The moment I date the image associated with the bird, twin impulses are created, what I would describe as the impulses of timeless imagination and timed imagination. The prefixes "meta-," "met-," and "meto-" are related and, according to several dictionaries of word roots, operate

Stellar's jay

on a continuum, generally meaning "beyond," "across," "between," or "change." "Metaphor": *Meta*, meaning between, across, after, or change. Plus *phor*, from *bher*, the Indo-European root meaning "to bear" or "to carry." A metaphor carries across or between. And "metonymy"—meta/meto, to change, plus *nym*, name. To change the name.

Most of us know what metaphors are, the comparison of unlike things, sometimes very different things. "The internet is his opium den." We use hundreds of them per day. The concept of metonymy is more slippery, though we use it every day also, hundreds of times. In a strict sense, it is a substitution of a part for the whole, or a substitution of something that is nearby. "The White House has made a statement." We substitute a house the person lives in for the person himself. "My heart is full." The heart substitutes for the feelings. "Let me lend you a hand." We are not lending an actual hand; we are lending help. Metonymy substitutes or replaces one thing for another that is beside it; one could say, it is a very local replacement, so in metonymy, images can follow one after another, and they don't "stand" for anything other than themselves, though one could make a philosophical claim that everything in metonymic writing stands for the world. But metaphors compare one thing to another, reaching clear into the unknown, the unseen, the imagined. They make the leap.

The linguist Roman Jakobson wrote a seminal essay on language and aphasia, "Two Aspects of Language and Two Types of Aphasic Disturbances"; he was one of the first to connect linguistic theory with actual brain function. He writes of the twofold nature of the loss of spoken language among aphasia patients he studied, and notes that there are two kinds of linguistic substitution that occur in his patients: those who have trouble selecting their words but don't have trouble arranging them ("combination and contexture"), and those who

have trouble arranging them but have no trouble se-
lecting ("selection and substitution"). I am of course rad-
ically simplifying; it's a fascinating essay worth looking
up. As Jakobson notes, metaphor and metonymy both
begin with impulses of substitution. He takes a step
further and applies these kinds of substitution to im-
pulses in literature. Metonymy has to do with realism
in literature, with contiguity, nearness, besideness, and
generally with linear connections we make in realist
prose, whereas metaphor has more to do with poetry,
especially with the Romantic and Symbolist traditions
of poetry. Jakobson suggests that many of our mental
events take place between the two poles, that creative
thought requires an energy between these functions,
and that these skills give our experience a kind of sub-
stance that is also an activity. Humans make linguistic
works of art through images, stories, and abstract ar-
rangements of words. Metaphors involve states of being
that leap into the unknown, whereas metonymy helps
us with the placement in time, history, story, and lin-
earity, a besideness as the sister skill no less important
to poets than is metaphor. I will borrow part of Jakob-
son's use of the metonymy as referring to impulses of
realism, besideness, storytelling in a loose and nontech-
nical sense.

In our daily lives, we constantly deploy either the

winged comparisons of metaphor or the sequential forms of metonymy. A farmer, speaking of a drought-ruined field: "It looks bare as a dance floor." Aristotle notes that metaphor consists in "giving the thing a name that belongs to something else." Writing without metaphoric images can be just as beautiful: blackbirds light in the field. The tractor drives through and the husks lie down in August, aslant.

Sometimes metaphor and metonymy seem very closely related and the distinctions blur. Poet Matthew Zapruder writes in *Why Poetry:* "Language is by its nature inherently metaphorical. Each word conceptually replaces something else: a thing, an idea, a phenomenon." Someone has a wild dream and recounts it in metaphors and symbols, but the syntax, story, and linearity sew the dream in place.

|  |  |  | ) | \ |  | \ |  |  |  |  | \ |  |  |  |  |

Here is a poem by Evie Shockley from her book *the new black.*

my last modernist poem #4
(or, re-re-birth of a nation)

a clean-cut man brings a brown blackness
to a dream-carved, unprecedented
place. some see in this the end of race

like the end of a race that begins
      with a gun: a finish(ed) line we might
finally limp across. for others,

      this miracle marks an end like year's
end, the kind that whips around again
      and again: an end that is chilling,
with a lethal spring coiled in the snow.

———————

        ask lazarus about miracles:
    the hard part comes afterwards. he stepped
        into the reconstruction of his
    life, knowing what would come, but not how.

This poem is packed with metaphor and metonymy. Though Obama's name is never mentioned, the historic election is rendered with resonant force in the "dream-carved, unprecedented / place." Shockley spoke recently at a Zoom poetry reading about "the way history keeps shadowing us and overshadowing us." You can see the play of metonymic shifts in the colors and shadows, the man bringing "a brown blackness." The poem goes from a first stanza that is relatively metaphor-free; to a word-play metaphor on race/race in the second stanza; to the third stanza, in which time is compared to a whip, an enjambed poetic line that visually whips around, and the implicit metaphor that history must be, as the title indicates, re-reborn. To accustom the reader to degrees of metaphor, the move of the last stanza is allegorical, which is an extreme form of symbolic metaphor: there is a line between the living and the dead, and below that line, Lazarus, not yet risen from the dead, waits to be asked about miracles, reconstruction/ Reconstruction, but the line is decidedly ironic. If you ask Lazarus about miracles, the hard part comes after. The line on the page allows the metonymic and the metaphoric to reside as story and image in the whiteness of the page. The metaphoric line, literally and figuratively, demarcates earth and presence. Human action must follow the miracle. Though a tone of foreboding is active, this poem opens a new zone for wonder and possibility.

|  |  |  |  |  \  |  \  |  |  |  |  |  \  \  |

Metaphors are born early, and so are our stories. Rilke points to childhood, to art, and to dreams as sources of poetry. Dreams are folded from a secret interior like egg

Portrait of Baudelaire by Étienne Carjat, c. 1862

whites into a soufflé. A great way to think of the role of metonymy is through one of its categories, synecdoche. Nineteen head of cattle, but we mean not just the head. In childhood, my brothers played baseball and I watched baseball. Baseball is perhaps the richest sport for this form of metonymy, the substitution of a part for the whole: The Giants need a new glove in right field (a guy holding a glove). The Giants need a new arm in the rotation (they need a new pitcher). The Giants could use an extra bat (a guy holding a bat, not just a bat all by itself).

I had to augment straight-up realism in my poetry because of poor eyesight beginning in early childhood. Stumps looked like coyotes, thistles were court jesters. Pieces of a busted tire looked like snakes in the road. Thus, metaphor-making was inevitable. When I had cataract surgery recently in my left eye, I asked the surgeon to leave some of my metaphors in the damaged eye; he said he would.

Baudelaire has always been important to me—his moody interior spaces. When I first read *Les Fleurs du mal* in college, I saw his symbolism came from the life force in the invisible world. His symbols provided a divine correspondence to the other world as powerful and necessary as salt. His poem "Correspondences" notes that we are only walking through a symbolic world.

### Correspondences

Nature is a temple in which living pillars
Sometimes allow confused words to come forth;
Man passes along through forests of symbols
That look at him with familiar eyes.

The search for the invisible through metaphor and the

process of the mind performing that activity corre-
spond for many writers to keeping childhood intact.

Maybe the difference between poets and other
people is that we are not really able to become normal
functioning adults but are doomed to fake it. Maybe
this is tied to our walking dream lives, but not only. We
remember being children at play, when allegory and
personification ruled the room, allowing the world to
be additionally inhabited so we were free from the anx-
ious adults. There is no reason to give up this practice:
moths can become souls, RNA strands become trav-
eling threads, the corona virus becomes a spiked ball
that looks like a Christmas ornament. Writers accom-
modate both metaphor and metonymy.

| | \ | | | \ | | | \ | | | \ |

C. D. Wright, a matchless inventor, produced an
abundance of poems across many styles. Her poetic
impulse sometimes seems primarily metonymic, in
that she piles images and narrative chunks next to each
other as if to describe lives and minds in a devotional
inventory, but her work also includes a boundless array
of metaphors. She was a close friend, and we often dis-
cussed our impatience with overly reductive rubrics
and categories in contemporary writing, including the
impulse to label modernist-inflected poetry in dispar-

aging terms. Her final book, *Shall Cross,* has a section of masterful short poems called "Forty Watts"; the title is a great metaphor in itself: a 40-watt bulb is not a strong bulb but is strong enough to read by, and produces a softer, more manageable lighting experience. Once we had a conversation about the difficulty of writing powerful stand-alone short poems as sequences of lyrics featuring process thinking. Each of the "Forty Watts" deploys short lists, catalogues, snatches of discontinuous events, incidents, and hallucinatory descriptions with such economy they read like unpunctuated narrative sketches for whole novels, each as a micro–dream diary with a waking image.

Here is a powerful example from the sequence.

## Poem Missing Someone

shielding her eyes from the sun
with her free hand stabbed by
the sudden thought of him
standing on the rim of some pond
wind washing the beans out of his dish
teaching a dog to retrieve in water
living within himself one lost valley

This haunting, tiny, unpunctuated poem has an endo-skeleton of participial phrases and gerunds: "shielding,"

"standing," "washing," "teaching," and "living." No com-
plete sentence is formed here, and the setting is an ap-
parently general outdoor scene: someone is standing
outside, shielding her eyes, thinking of another person
on the rim "of some pond," seemingly beside his own
life, washing a dish, teaching a dog. In an implied met-
aphor in the second line, the hand of the thinker is
"stabbed" by a thought. Then there is a more explicit
metaphor at the end, and when it arrives, it simultane-
ously weighs the piece down and buoys it: "living within
himself one lost valley," a striking image of a solitary
figure with an unknowable soul. The words "one lost
valley" conflate the mysteries in the person with a pow-
erful depth charge in a missing landscape. Like a painter
quickly switching from a favorite color to a new palette,
this poet is a spirit in a hurry, and the poem honors
time and timelessness in its conveyance of an intense
lyric experience. This is one of the most powerful things
a metaphor can do in the context of a small story; like
the lemon wheels in the Ritsos piece, the image of the
lost valley renders a story of yearning and of something
fundamentally irretrievable.

| \ | | | | | | \ | | | | | | | \ |

Metaphor asks two things to coexist in the mind,

Laura and Daniel Kinney, and Brad, Brenda, and Brent Hillman,
c. 1959, Tucson, Arizona

not unlike a pun, not unlike Wallace Stevens's "mon-
ocle de mon oncle." In metonymy's besideness, you can
have sequential heres and theres. Both devices make
strangeness possible. Viktor Shklovsky suggests the
essential function of poetic art is to counteract habit-
uation, to defamiliarize so that we end up really seeing
the world instead of dumbly recognizing it. Story-mind,
or even syntax-mind, an experience or a history or just
the story of a sentence telling itself, can certainly also
defamiliarize. Our job is to renegotiate styles of reality.
Remember how we tried hard to be normal when we

were children? Most children have both metaphoric and metonymic relationships to consciousness. In those early, undifferentiated zones, things took place simultaneously, yet time passed. There were glimpses of wholeness, as if our families had always been happy, as if we had praise at the right time.

Myths retain their truths if you metaphorize them. I grew up in the Sonoran desert, the middle child of fervently Protestant parents raised by fervent Protestants. Stories like those of Lazarus were told as the historical truth. Hard to say whether the story or the image of Lazarus was odder, which is why I love Evie Shockley's rendering of Lazarus, safe below the line. I decided in adolescence to rescue the Judeo-Christian tradition from itself, which involved seeing many earthly practices as metaphoric. There is, for example, church communion, which Baptists call "The Lord's Supper." Children taking Christian communion, when they come to consciousness, realize that the practice involves the astonishing and the weird because of the premise of eating the body and drinking the blood. At our Baptist church, Nabisco Saltine crackers were used in communion. The deity was both a cracker and an invisible spirit, a fact to be continuously renegotiated. My brothers and I would peer down into steel trays filled with tiny pieces of Saltines and watch as trays with the delicate fluted glasses of Welch's grape juice shook and rattled. It's unclear why Baptists used Saltine crackers; possibly bread would be considered too Catholic, and certainly an elite object like a wafer would seem too Lutheran, which was far too close to Catholic. Jesus lived in the invisible realm, far away; the Saltine cracker, representing his body, was very local. My mother, wearing white gloves, had an ability to pick up the tiniest piece of cracker, about a half-inch square, with her glove and get it successfully to her mouth without a single crumb falling onto her immaculate lap. My theory was she chose the smallest piece out of self-sacrifice and the larger, inch-sized pieces were left for others.

Maybe the historical Jesus had some ability to stream electrical energy from his hands and to perform miracles; we just don't know. This electrical flow from nature resonated when I read Wordsworth and Whitman later. I became what is now called an "episco-pagan," incorporating the druidic plant, animal, and ancestor worship into the part of the Christian tradition I retained. Whenever I hear *body of Christ, bread of heaven* in mass, I still think Jesus is at least in part a Nabisco Saltine washed down with Welch's grape juice. I'm taken back to Tucson, 1959, my mother is sitting beside me; her white gloves are as real as they can be in my memory, little ridges with prominent white thread. My mother is not a metaphor for anything—she is the essence of the real. The Saltine cracker, the Jesus body, the mother all reside in my same few brain cells. Remember the distinctions from Jakobson. Metonymy is our skill with close relations to reality, the arranging function. Metaphor. Meta + phor—the carrier of the after, the invisible, the later.

l l l l \ l l l l l l ) \ l \ l l

A current practitioner of great poetic force is Tongo Eisen-Martin. In his writing, metaphoric thought and metonymy abound in lines of tremendous power. The title poem of his collection *Heaven Is All Goodbyes* renders an account of the poet and his brother traveling to take their father's ashes across the country. The poem is long so I'll share twenty lines from the beginning and the end.

### Heaven Is All Goodbyes

A 1978 statement

My brother Biko and I are driving
In an empty cell lane

We are God's evil to these settlers
They might throw us under the shift change

We take wolf naps
We don't know what else we good at besides this traveling

State lines in a night tide passing through beachhead america
Passing with hurricane memory

—Three thousand exits of sludge-bathed apartheid

Everything south of canada is extrajudicial gun oil
And your local unemployment factory

In a few hours we will fit in          Relax for now

Hop out of the car and I'm a dirty shoe illusion
Leaning on the trunk with the ghosts of switchblades
                                        And other rusty services

I am enemy humor
And traveling

Father's ashes on the back seat behind two sons

                    In a lane not for metaphor
Well, maybe a metaphor about something unfinished
        —One million hands passing us through the Midwest

. . . . . .

Barreling like gut born love songs
Your ancestors are smiling
As we pass the time
When we ride
It's language

Passed Gary 3000
Cast iron lining / Proud forearms for meals

Three-man ghost story

Fishers of ourselves

Cards dealt

Narrative implied

Maybe something unfinished

Like an Indiana hurricane
Or two midnights in Milwaukee

Or no arms
No tattoos
No Chicago
Ever again

We don't know what else we good at
Besides this traveling

And besides
Heaven is all goodbyes
Anyway

Eisen-Martin's poems have become iconic for fearlessly braiding scenes and tones; they fuse disparate images, from the most surreal and hallucinatory to the stark pickup sticks of urban landscapes. This poem places recognizable elements of realist observation against a background saturated with sensory color. Bits of crisp monosyllabic sounds—"cell lane," "shift change," "wolf naps"—are collaged in a blur that makes up an American road trip, a solid yet contingent world. The

poet deploys choruses of collective voices in a con-
trapuntal way in a complex narrative structure; his
fast-shifting, dialectical style draws in both metaphor
and recognizable reference from midwestern land-
scapes. As the two brothers drive the ashes of their fa-
ther across the country's economically depressed and
toxically racialized landscapes, the states of America
seem metonymic, lined up and beside. The narrative's
paratactic techniques allow the *besideness* to unfold
with visual and auditory elements; the central image—
"Father's ashes on the back seat between two sons"—is
both metaphoric and metonymic, as the ashes become
a stand-in for the father's body, transported across the
states. The poet notes in line twenty that he will employ
metaphor among his other devices, and the metaphors
pile up brilliantly and tautologically: "In a lane not for
metaphor / Well, maybe a metaphor about something
unfinished /—One million hands passing us through
the Midwest." The poem performs itself through a series
of metaphors for illusion and movement, yet the engine
of the poem is the deeply moving, unsentimental sto-
rytelling made powerful by the seamless action taking
place between the dominant threads of the lines. Eisen-
Martin's metaphors allow story, community, and sub-
jectivity to align. On tenterhooks, a tender journey, a
"father's last trip home," a journey fraught with turns,

the voice that is at times oracular and at times plain makes bridges across types of thought. In the journey, the poet ruefully observes several times that "We don't know what else we good at besides this traveling," as if to give further permission for the flecks of dreamy realism, process thinking, and estranged grammar that take place in a world of perilous beauty and singular peril.

| | | | | \ | | | \ | | | | ) \ |

As a poet, I am driven by metaphors, personal, mythic, collective—*here, two beyonds in the same place as*—but I am tethered by the movement through time, *next, next, beside, beside.* Parking meters simultaneously produce the thought of herons. Every day, we are sustained by images. An undergraduate student writes in his first poem about looking in a mirror: "I spray a golf-ball of mousse on my hand." His daily hair routine helper appears as a little foamy golf ball. A friend said, of her children: "Every time I ask them to clean their rooms, it's like sending them to Siberian labor camp." On the relaxation tape: "Your neck muscles should feel just like a bunch of loose rubber bands." Walt Whitman, rarely a grouch about writing, remarked in his notebook, " It seems to me necessary to avoid all poetical similes to be faithful to perfect likelihoods of nature," and yet he claims in part 7 of *Song of Myself* that his big soul is as "stout as a horse," asserting himself through metaphor, linking himself through metonymy: "I am not an earth nor an adjunct of an earth, / I am the mate and companion of people, all just as immortal and fathomless as myself." If, as Freud claims, the capacity to make images in dreams is not only innate but compresses necessary desire or displacement of desire, when we wake, we arrange those images, give them context, sweep them in. Freud's sometime colleague and rival Carl Jung writes in *Memories, Dreams, Reflections* that every story of trauma or wish rhymes with mythic remnants called archetypes that connect our experiences to those of others; he writes of his career choice: "The collision of nature and spirit became a reality. . . . It was as though two rivers had united and in one grand torrent were bearing me inexorably toward distant goals. This confident feeling that I was a 'united double nature' carried me as if on a magical wave through the examination." When I first read this passage, I was struck by the idea of united double nature. Jung accommodates his opposites—light and dark, male and female, spirit and matter—permitting a nonbinary, nonoppositional dynamic that allows his creativity to function better in times of unmanageable turbulence. This idea can carry

Great blue heron

us in an existence that is communal and mysterious, even with painful emotions of ancestors in our historical consciousness. The creative soul is often built on paradox, on what is quirky or unappealing, merely puzzling or unrecognizable, and on what gives comfort or ease as our patterns of perception flow between what recurs and what does not return.

| | | | \ | | | | | ) \ | | \ |

A few years ago, Bob and I gave several talks on the role of poetry in the peace process—a big topic. At one such gathering in Korea, I spoke about how metaphor demonstrates one thing and acknowledges the imposition of the other at the same time. It is like sitting at the peace table where nonviolent mediation might work in international diplomacy or even in family mediation during a misunderstanding. People who hold opposite views and who ascribe to unlike goals must sit at the same table, in the space of time, and come to an agreement. The mediation table is a space of animated emptiness. Metaphor and the practice of nonviolence thus have something in common. Metaphor is built on this paradox, and metonymy asks that observations be related in time. Metaphor and metonymy, the *instead* and the *beside*, sit so close to each other in life that it is impossible to untangle them. A poem swirls its symbolic expressions around a great silence and must accommodate itself to the processes and the negations of its making, taking the absence of the "other" into itself, making very interior mental processes available to—and at least somewhat accessible to—the external world. If the job of a metaphoric impulse is to put things together that never thought they could speak to each other, maybe the job of the arranger, the metonymic impulse, is to be reasonable, to bear reality, quivering and shaking, to and away from the table. I have thought of this many times in the terribly noncollaborative years we've just lived through politically.

Two more poems in tonight's talk. Layli Long Soldier's remarkable first book of poetry, *Whereas,* was written in response to the 2009 Congressional Resolution of Apology to Native Americans, which President Obama signed. Long Soldier is a dual citizen of the Oglala Lakota Nation and the United States. The brilliant title poem deploys the word "whereas" at the beginning of each of its many sections, and quite often within sections at the beginnings of lines or clauses; this device is anaphora, of course, and it also constructs and stitches together the language of the central metaphor: a resolution or agreement that has failed to accomplish its goals. Here is the third section in which she presents an understated account of an incident, with an extended metaphor.

> WHEREAS at four years old I read the first chapter of the
> Bible aloud I was not Christian
>
> Whereas my hair unbraided ran the length of my spine
> I sometimes sat on it
>
> Whereas at the table my legs dangled I could not balance
> peas on my fork

Whereas I used my fingers carefully I pushed the bright
    green onto the silver tines

Whereas you eat like a pig the lady said setting my plate
    on the floor

Whereas she instructed me to finish on my hands and
    knees she took another bite

Whereas I watched folds of pale curtains inhale and
    exhale a summer dance

Whereas in the breath of the afternoon room each tick
    of the clock

Whereas I rose and placed my eyes and tongue on a shelf
    above the table first

Whereas I kneeled to my plate I kneeled to the greatest
    questions

Whereas that moment I knew who I was whereas the
    moment before I swallowed . . .

The use of the term "Whereas" as a title is the book's central presiding metaphor; a "Whereas" is a device commonly used in legal documents, contracts, or resolutions instead of the word "because." As soon as the catalogue begins, we understand the interrogation of the legal contract takes place in the realm of personal and family story, ancestral history of Indigenous nations in general and of the Oglala Lakota Nation in particular. The incidents in Long Soldier's poem are either apparently personal and individual or apparently tribal. The anaphoric use of "whereas" is a kind of metaphoric hinge for causality that will have no consequence except the assertion of poetic truth. The tone the metaphor of a legal document creates is ironic—sometimes lightly ironic, and sometimes bitterly. The fact of trying to ironize the nonbindingness of the resolution creates a relentless quality, an epic recitation of cumulative historical harm not ameliorated at all by a congressional resolution of apology for centuries of abuse and neglect. There are other kinds of metaphor and metonymy in this section as well. The human child is fed like a dog, an image presented flatly and without drama. The afternoon has breath. The curtains are animated and dance in a personified way. There is an extreme moment of disembodiment when the child-self of the poet speaker places "my eyes and tongue on a shelf above the table first"; the catalogue of actions is given no ranking in this selection. Throughout this powerful work, Long Soldier often assembles examples from nonhuman species and things. The anaphora of "Whereas" continues to draw the reader into a kind of an anti-treaty in which individual harm precludes the possibility of restorative justice.

| ) | | | \ | ) \ \ | | | | | |

The last poem of metaphor and metonymy is "Motive for Metaphor," one of my favorite poems by Wallace Stevens. It describes the "haunting by otherness" that Keats calls negative capability, the act of entering a perceptual field with a sense of egoless imaginative willingness. Here is the whole poem.

### The Motive for Metaphor

You like it under the trees in autumn,
Because everything is half dead.
The wind moves like a cripple among the leaves
And repeats words without meaning.

In the same way, you were happy in spring,
With the half colors of quarter-things,
The slightly brighter sky, the melting clouds,
The single bird, the obscure moon—

The obscure moon lighting an obscure world
Of things that would never be quite expressed,
Where you yourself were not quite yourself,
And did not want nor have to be,

Desiring the exhilarations of changes:
The motive for metaphor, shrinking from
The weight of primary noon,

The A B C of being,

The ruddy temper, the hammer
Of red and blue, the hard sound—
Steel against intimation—the sharp flash,
The vital, arrogant, fatal, dominant X.

When I first read this poem in my twenties, I thought it provided an impossible instruction manual for writers and other sensitive souls. *How* could you "like it under trees in autumn," not just when everything is half dead but *because* everything is half dead? The *you* has the same problem in spring, with the "half-colors of quarter things"; the *you* is somehow made happier by being partial than they would by being complete. Stevens takes us to the root of the creative act, making metaphor metonymically, in time, as time passes, out of a state of pre- or non- or unfulfillment rather than from fulfillment. There are many discussions of this poem by critics and poets. What does he mean by the "vital, arrogant, fatal, dominant X"? Some read it as the objective world, the universal "givens" outside the self. I've always read it to mean what we cannot transform by metaphor.

A note about the writer before I go further: Stevens was a successful, white, upper-middle-class businessman, a modernist of deeply strange and philosophically inward inventions. I wish to note that, by several accounts, he made racist remarks about the poet Gwendolyn Brooks. I will never forgive him for that and acknowledge it as historical fact. I teach Stevens's poetry anyway, believing that great art can exist despite the terrible behavior of its flawed maker in a racist world that has yet to be redeemed. If we did not accept and call out the imperfections of the makers, no great art would survive. And this poem claims that there are lots of *inspite of*s in the act of making, implying that the imaginative person is different from most people, making life from impossible paradoxes, making the visible from invisible, accepting shifts and abstraction as part of the task. The world cannot slow down long enough to read your poetry, but you have a commitment to the half-color of quarter things; accepting this impossibly partial state and doing the deed of making anyway is an enigma that drives the creative soul to do what it does.

In closing I'll note that when I believe I cannot bear the grief of the Anthropocene anymore, I think of some hidden idea and/or fact of other species, of the spiders, the extremophiles, the kingfisher, the finches, the grasses, the tides and sea mammals, even those at risk. I think of foxes in our area, including the one who comes to visit our yard, in their dens; of marmots in the Sierra peaks that will see no human, deep in winter; of the be-

Inverness fox

sideness of so many species becoming devastated; and the moth of history flutters in my garden. I refuse to identify only with my species; humans are only one species of 8,700,000. When I studied lichen species thinking about metaphor, I learned how some species grow only a centimeter in a hundred years. They can still be themselves, moving very slowly through time, living on light, water, and air, with no official root system. In my trance work and in my studies of lichen, I think about the many colors of this skin of earth. When I'm horrified by every form of violence humans commit against other humans and the planet, I'm sustained by thinking of the life beyond the small local Brenda life in which ego betrays my soul. I am finishing this talk ten months after I started it; this is a month when the Capitol building is being stormed by white supremacists protesting the outcome of the election.

For each of my three talks I'll give you some homework: I encourage you to develop your habit of being a walking dreamer, with one foot inside daily life, to cultivate straddling multiple associations and kinds of time. Do not let imagination be trained out of you this week as you spend too much brain-deadening time on social media. My wish for us all, especially those of us who think constantly about social ills, is that we use acts of imagination to get us through without despair, forming relationships to otherness, to dream or vision and metaphor, with a metonymic relationship to realism, connectedness and besideness, to constitute a shared grammar of reality that moves from the unknown to the known, or the known to the unknown or the unknown to the unknown with metonymy and metaphor, justice and love.

# MEANING
## *and*
# MYSTERY


IT IS 1968. I am in the desert at night with my friend X. We are both counterculture hippies dressed in blue satin clothing, talking about talking to the dead. He thinks the spirits are far away, I think they are close by. X is an expert in theosophy, astrology, the astral plane. Waves of desert insect sounds recede like rows of parentheses. The Tucson mountains give a sense of mystical protection, the glittering in the rocks and the stars. By day, I am a good student, aware of my gender, not very awake to my whiteness. To appease my stoner friends, I am growing a cannabis plant in the back yard that doubles as a house plant; I tell my mother it is called a "false aralia." I've been reading poetry: Denise Levertov, Kenneth Patchen, e. e. cummings. My class-mates and I are flower children, we use sealing wax

Sunset in rainy season, Tucson, Arizona, 2016

on our letters; in senior year we will be protesting war
and racism, listening to Dylan, the Doors, and Marvin
Gaye in tents. The freedom of revolt, the freedom of

The author's bookshelf

the body, the freedom of poetry merge in us, against adult rationality.

Half a century later, there is a tiny hissing sound of an insect near my computer. Millions of brain cells spring to their heuristic task. It is not an insect but the top of my thermos bottle. Nearby, images of my mother, of Mahershala Ali and Alex Hibbert in *Moonlight*, the young Barbara Guest, of Bert and Ernie. I think of the night with X in the desert when, facing my bookshelf: California lichens, Dickinson's letters, the Communist Manifesto, John Keats, spiders and mayflies, Noam Chomsky, the Bible, a book of Indo-

European roots and some of X's books about the hermetic arts, clairvoyance, Arcana Mundi, casting spells, witchcraft, theosophy, and alchemy. A few years after our night meeting in the desert, X declares he is finished with all that, joins a fundamentalist church, brings me his books and his silver jewelry and disappears to California to take a job in a secret agency. I am grateful to him for what I took to be his vast knowledge.

| | | | | ) \ | \ | | \ | | | |

All year during the pandemic I have been thinking about making meaning of experience, especially the bafflement of collective suffering, and how we make meaning in poetry. Last week I spoke about how metaphor and metonymy are not adversarial factors but are compatible engagements with reality, dizygotic twins in our imaginations. Tonight I will continue trampling down the vintage where poetic binaries are stored, to muse on another dyad, Meaning and Mystery; such large concepts, and we will barely have time for a few glimmerings in the poems and experiences I will share.

The Jungian psychologist James Hillman, no relation, notes that the meaning-making function is Psyche, the soul, the sorter of seeds. The soul is a metaphor for a process of making meaning, including the states of depression and emotional struggle. The Indo-European root of the word "meaning" is *mei-no,* which means "opinion or intention." The word "moaning" also stems from *mei-no;* perhaps finding a meaning in life is akin to finding a moaning. The word "mystery" has two possible Indo-European roots: one is *meuə*—"to be silent"; the other root is *mei,* meaning "small." I will offer examples to show how meaning and mystery—also forces of imagination, what is intended and what is held in secret—make fine dance partners.

❘ \ ❘ ❘ ❘ ❘ ❘ \ ❘ ❘ ❘ ❘ ❘ ❘ \ ❘

People are often baffled about poetry and want to know how to engage with it; they are convinced it is packed with secret meanings the author intended but that they have no access to. Matthew Zapruder in *Why Poetry* notes: "Unlike other forms of writing, poetry takes as its primary task to insist and depend upon and celebrate the troubled relation of the word to what it represents." Barbara Guest writes in *Forces of Imagination:* "Coleridge said that a poem must be both *obscure* and *clear.* This is what we search for in our poem, this beautiful balance between *the hidden and the open.*"

Several decades back, there were earnest essays by poets defending and critiquing "difficulty" in poetry. "Difficulty" sounded as if poets were engaged in a distasteful medical procedure and referred mostly to modernist practice, by now as old as Baudelaire. Baudelaire, whom I saluted last week, is considered by some to be the first modern poet; in the 1850s he introduced the world to mood-driven poetry of atmospheres and symbols, to subjects that hadn't been considered poetic, including mental anxiety and life in the underbelly of cities. Baudelaire was not trying to be difficult; he was writing of life as a modern man. Tonight I will mostly use the word *mystery* instead of the word *difficulty*.

Unlike many people, I think about the Big Bang nearly every day. Why did it happen? Time and space were threaded through the quantum of nothingness. Was there a slight ticking right before the beginning, like when you turn off your car after a long drive? Stars are being forced out; minutes are forming. Billions of years pass. The four strands of the RNA, the polymeric molecule, cook in warm pools. Billions of years pass again. Suddenly there are Chihuahuas, bran flakes, clouds, humans, and the big yellow fungus I pass on my walk. Existence is so peculiar. As Elizabeth Bishop writes, "How unlikely!" And now they've discovered a particle that may lead to a fifth dimension. The co-

Fungus, possibly Laetiporus gilbertsonii (thank you to my brother
Brad Hillman and to Mark Conway for the identification)

rona virus, a spiked protein, is evil for some but not all. *Evil* is *live* spelled backward. *Mystery* and *meaning* spin through the lobes of our brains, the frontal, the parietal, the occipital and temporal, into the limbic zones.

Meaning is on a hunt within us, like an owl that rarely sleeps.

| | | | | | | | | \ \ | \ | \ |

I'm interested in the moment in a poem right before it is understood. Some mysteries in poems connect to daily silences, what poet-lawyer Pat Gilbert called "the immersion in the unremarkable, its simple intricacy," and there are as many kinds of meanings and mysteries as there are works of art. I think of Ezra Pound's three principles of poetry: (1) *logopoeia,* words experienced through their denotative meanings; (2) *phanopoeia,* images that take the reader into a set of collective image associations; and (3) *melopoeia,* the sound properties of language itself. I would add (4) *biopoeia*—the life force in the poem—events, historical contexts, ideas, materials, one might even say "subject matter." Connections are made in us when we hear a poem for the first time. A poem is a box. You can see the front corners, but the back corners are always hidden.

| | | | \ | | | | | | \ | ) \ |

Here is poem by Simone White remarkable for its phrasal power and lexical complexity (*logopoeia*) as well as for its life-force (*biopoeia*).

## There was a time I hardly went three steps

Except another black girl was with me.

Mother. Always lonely. I am always.
Mother those girls. Forty-two.

March summer. Light blue. Vermont.
Endless crescent. Invert as a tyke lake.

Fernet Mother, I'm grown. Forest.
San Francisco. Lone cold.

Stone turd. Talk three or none.
Kidding.
Kidding.

This mysterious and appealing piece shares its first four words with an iconic nineteenth century British poem, Wordsworth's "Ode: Intimations on Immortality," the first lines of which are, "There was a time when meadow, grove, and stream, / The earth, and every common sight, / To me did seem / Appareled in celestial light." White also enters her poem with unclouded iambic pentameter. She offers a compressed and fragmentary recollection via collaged staccato phrases, inverted grammatical structures and short declarative sentences. This sort of poetic mystery, however, is not one of omission but of selection, a layering of brief flashbacks. The couplet "Mother. Always lonely. I am always. / Mother those girls. Forty-two" gives a great deal of information in pointillist fashion: one word, then a period, then two words, then a period, three words then a period. The next line ("Mother those girls. Forty-two") could be an imperative or a description. The poem's lyric compression allows meaning to emerge, sometimes by shorthand, even suggesting encoded childhood speech that becomes a memorable surreal image: "Stone turd. Talk three or none. / Kidding. / Kidding." It's the kind of thing a kid says to herself as a secret marker, and the verb "kidding" underscores the "kid." The poem takes place across a span of time in several landscapes, including Vermont and San Francisco, and the poet doesn't need us to follow every step. Personal associations of mothering and childhood are intertwined by means of grammatical inversions, suggesting that shared experiences sometimes produce more loneliness for the mother and at other times more loneliness for the child. If a poem could be paraphrased, the *biopoeia* aspect of this poem might fill in: "I'm remembering when you were forty-two . . . we were in Vermont . . . the experience of looking at a shape on a lake . . . reminds me of other times in my life I feel lonely . . ." White's carefully delineated word-world supports the need to honor the mystery of an experience. The poet's aesthetic decisions intensify the mystery of experience through evocation as the meanings are displayed bit by bit, with compression and economy.

| | | | \ | | | | | ) | \ | \ |

Sometimes at a poetry reading, a grouchy person will ask during a Q and A, "Why can't poets just say things directly?" My answers occasionally include the question: What do you mean by directly? In fact, fragmentary poems can be very direct, each fragment flintlike or a shard of energy. Most of people's days are made of fragments. When we are at the market, we rarely think in grammatically complete sentences: "I hope to find the perfect eggplant"; we think, "small eggplant." The varied music inside our heads includes the bumpy and the smooth. Then the grouchy person asks, "Don't you care if I know what you're trying to convey?" They might feel left out of compressed, allusive, or disjunctive styles. While I don't blame them for their impatience, I try to tell them their poetry education was incomplete, that modernism is a hundred years old, that sometimes their tired teachers chose poems that would have impact after one reading. Poetry like Simone White's emerges from a different mental pacing; she's capable of smoothness, as her title suggests, but she resists offering the smooth account because that is not what the experience of memory is in this case. Such poems grow richer and deeper with multiple visits. Let us keep appreciating the compression in poetry. In the culinary arts, delicious sauces are often made by boiling down a liquid. Such sauces are called "reductions"; they are not called "difficult" sauces.

| | | | \ | | | | | ) | \ | \ |

In the decades after X gave me his books on the occult, I learned that myth, spiritual practices, and poetic practices all share processes of interactive interpretation. "Meaning" is created by a process, not by exact measure; it is not that the maker has poured in a half cup of meaning and we must extract the same half cup. We add to the experience of meaning each time we give the works our attention and love. Barbara Guest describes this: "Do you ever notice as you write that no matter what is there on the written page something appears to be *in back of everything that is said, a little ghost*? I judge that this ghost is there to remind us there is always more, and elsewhere, a hiddenness, a secondary form of speech." There is pleasure in this quality of hiddenness even if much seems apparent on a first reading. What is "really there" when you are finding meaning in a poem? In 1968, I wanted to know if the dead were "really there"; over the next few decades, under the guidance of healers and on my own, I developed a trance practice when I needed spiritual sustenance. Some of my foundational poets—Blake, Yeats, H.D., Robert Duncan and other San Francisco Renaissance Poets—had engaged in forms of vision work. I began to study Gnostic, esoteric, and alchemical writings to engage with more inclusive spiritualities. I have often referred to the books X gave me, including the theosophical writings of Annie Besant, to develop techniques for going into the zones of poetic imagination. I do not see the visionary in opposition to rational models or scientific ones. Nearly four decades later I still use trance hours for inner searches and processes. When writing a quartet of books on earth, air, water, and fire, I did small daily rituals with the elements. In 2006, while writing a long poem about California watershed regions I traced drops of water from their origins to their outlets. In the case of my own watershed, I made physical, mental, and digital journeys along the Mokelumne River, the source of my water, from its point of origins to my water glass, and did this for several other watersheds, including the Los Angeles watershed.

| ) | | | \ | | | | \ | | | \ |

Two days after the lockdown began in March 2020, my inbox began to house requests for poems that would comfort people. When people seek poems to ease the mystery of suffering, they might want what they call "accessible" poems. The whole issue is vexed. What makes modernist writing rewarding is in part what makes it difficult. Some blame T. S. Eliot specifically—and modernism generally—for making poetry difficult with his *Waste Land* in 1922. Also in 1922, Vallejo published *Trilce*; in 1923 Jean Toomer published *Cane*, Stevens published *Harmonium*. Modernism didn't lose audiences, it created new ones.

"April is the cruelest month" is certainly a mysterious opening line; hmm, March and February may be crueler. "Breeding / lilacs out of the dead land, mixing / memory and desire, stirring / dull roots with spring rain." The participles drip strangely off the ends of the lines like wisteria. That's weird, one of my undergraduates remarks. Who thinks the lovely month of April is cruel? Who is talking, my students ask? It always surprises me that they can watch hours of collage and montage techniques in Super Bowl commercials yet balk at the same techniques in a poem. *The Waste Land* is not inaccessible. It is a collaged, fragmentary poem about loneliness, urban alienation, and sexual unhappiness, about being out of touch with the spirit and the body, about environmental degradation— a great symphony of voices, devastatingly emotional; its tonal path is not straight or particularly easy. From modernism for the rest of the century, there would be more singing or less, more feeling or less, more reference or less; modernist styles will produce joy in some readers, bafflement and fear of feeling wrong in others, but *The Waste Land* is a great poem to read together anytime, especially during the pandemic. In the fall of 2019 during the California wildfires, my students and I sat in a room without electricity and read the poem by the light of our phones, each student taking a different voice, through the polyphonic wilderness: the depressed protagonist, the vatic father, the neurasthenic woman, the furtive sexual seeker, the drowned maidens, "Datta. Dayadhvam. Damyata" behind the thunder. Reading an intricate poem aloud together is a great gift. Sometimes indirection and disjunction help the crisis of the eternal *Now*. In modernist art and poetry, you will hear the undertow of the twentieth century that gave us some of our most mysterious answers.

| | | | | \ | \ | | | | | \ |

Even the most apparently clear poems can be mysterious. Robert Hass's work is known for its luminous clarity but it's sometimes an elusive clarity, like the surfaces of Vermeer; here is a short poem from *Praise*.

### To a Reader

I've watched memory wound you.
I felt nothing but envy.
Having slept in wet meadows,
I was not through desiring.
Imagine January and the beach,
a bleached sky, gulls. And
look seaward: what is not there
is there, isn't it, the huge
bird of the first light
arched above the first waters
beyond our touching or intention
or the reasonable shore.

Our reader enters a scene of shadowy beauty in progress. Something has been going on between the speaker and the *you*, something that caused the speaker "envy," the telling of a narrative or emotion. The first two statements are deceptively simple, a bit cryptic: "I've watched memory wound you. / I felt nothing but envy." The question of who is speaking is the first mystery here, a mystery not created by wordplay (*logopoeia*), syntactic oddities, or musical effects (*melopoeia*). The main device of the poem is *phanopoeia*, an image of a large bird of dawn, with a hint of Stevens's "Of Mere Being"; perhaps that bird exists "beyond our touching or intention." In a different way from Stevens's bird of fire-fangled feathers, this is an unnamed bird with a mythic largesse. The poem's *biopoeia* shares a state of mind in relation to a landscape in five declarative sentences that increase in length. We are plunged behind a shroud of mystery between two people, and the presence of a looming, strange embodiment hovering in the nonhuman world. The gentle but absolute tonal detachment creates a depth charge the way some of Rilke's poems do, in part through restraint; I'm thinking of "Herbsttag," "Autumn Day" in English, the opening of which Galway Kinnell translates as, "Lord: it is time. The summer was immense. / Lay your shadow on the sundials / and let loose the wind in the fields." In a workshop in the 1970s, Robert Hass might be asked to supply more information, yet more information is not needed to create the effect of the poem. The poet has overheard something at the center of his being and delivers it sparely. He leaves us with the incomplete. Can we find beauty in what is left hanging and accept that in some poems there is neither too much subjectivity nor too little? "To a Reader" is neither a "difficult" nor an "easy" poem.

I was in touch with Robert Hass recently (a little joke) and was informed that some material had been removed from the beginning. I asked him if he'd be willing to supply the original lines so I could share them with you. He remembers them this way:

> Grief takes on form, doesn't it?
> And the wise bamboo is just that.
> And a poem is a poem. Neither
> animals nor art, we go on, don't we?
> And perish at the end. Like the Hittites.
> Thin air. A fool and his money.

Boldly, I proposed that the removed lines could make another short cryptic poem; we will see if that poet follows my suggestion.

"To a Reader" creates a fertile zone of full nothingness between the poet and the mask, the persona. A "persona" in Greek theater refers to the mask that actors spoke through. "Person" comes from persona. You are always speaking *through* your personality, always wearing a mask. Once I asked Czeslaw Milosz who was speaking in his poems; he answered, "Brenda, it is always a mask!" Through the pandemic time, there has been one consistent message: wear your mask! The poet cannot help but comply.

|   |   |   |   |   |   \   |   \   |   |   |   |   |   )   \   |

Brenda Hillman in mask

One kind of mysterious meaning can be found in nursery rhymes and abstractly musical poems. Children learn musical semi-sense through nursery rhymes. Here is a passage from Lewis Carroll's poem "Jabberwocky."

'Twas brillig, and the slithy toves
Did gyre and gimble in the wabe:

All mimsy were the borogoves,
And the mome raths outgrabe.

Pure musical sense associations in "Jabberwocky" produce meanings that are "almost" meanings, perhaps because of the Disney cartoon with animals dancing "in the wabe." The words are almost words. This property of almost sense, of abstract sense, became a great fact of creative language introduced by Gertrude Stein, the French OuLiPo, John Ashbery, and Language poetry. Poetry became a site for invention and delight more than for personal revelation, and one of the main gifts of this period, especially of Language poetry, is to experience words as material, conveying emotion and association no matter what, necessarily polyphonic and collective. Some poets in the last several decades have valued collaboration over psychological exploration or accounts of family drama because language itself is endless and is a collective oracle. Yet many poets still approach poetry through the need for self-expression; the impact of more abstract poetry, even a hundred years after Stein, still feels radical. For all the writing students out there, the perceived divisions between expressive, lyric, and narrative traditions on the one hand and more material, abstract traditions on the other have broken down a great deal in the last few decades. More freedom is offered to you now because of things your ancestor poets have tried in order to be bold. We cannot disregard what sacrifices have been made in order to create new works.

The poet C. D. Wright and I often spoke about how lyric is infinitely mutable because lyric is not a genre but a quality. I even call it a flavor that pervades the universe. When I moved to the Bay Area in the 1970s, there was a vibrant experimental women's writing community, inspired somewhat by Objectivist writing, Black Mountain, and San Francisco Renaissance writers, but enacting these traditions through women's experience. (Shout out to Kathleen Fraser and Diane di Prima in poetry heaven, and to Patricia Dienstfrey, to Norma Cole, to other innovative poetic sisters of the time.) Writing during those decades was a great adventure. The possibilities for poetry exploded to include more process, "nonpoetic" materials, non sequitur, and polyphonic voices, inventions in formatting, hybrid genres, and subject matter. Poems were made of marginalia, on the back of grocery receipts, written in a twilight sleep. For some of us, trying new forms, this freedom was intensified across uneven surfaces all over the page, and included myth, politics, history, ecology, and other sciences directly from the heart in lyric forms. How a poem means has changed drastically.

One of the most important books of poetry to come out of that time was Harryette Mullen's book length poem *Muse and Drudge*. It remains as close to a visionary collective text as the twentieth century could produce. Mullen has noted she hoped to "pursue what is minor, marginal, idiosyncratic, trivial, debased or aberrant in the language I speak and write." Here is single page.

> why these blues come from us
> threadbare material soils
> the original colored
> pregnant with heavenly spirit
>
> stop running from the gift
> slow down to catch up with it
> knots mend the string quilt
> of kente stripped when kin split
>
> white covers of black material
> dense fabric that obeys its own logic
> shadows pieced together tears and all
> unfurling sheets of bluish music
>
> burning cloth in a public place
> a crime against the state
> raised the cost of free expression
> smoke rose to offer a blessing

In *Muse and Drudge* Mullen does not reject reference, metaphors, or lyric utterance; she brings the depths of Black cultural history into each quatrain by deploying grammatically incomplete fragments that are both personal and representative: "why these blues come from us" can be read as a sentence fragment, as can the next three lines, "threadbare material soils," "the original colored," and "pregnant with heavenly spirit." But the range of tones—querulous, elegiac, ironizing, then meditative—carries emotion. Every stanza and page of her text could be read as an independent unpunctuated poem with the whole comprising a georgic of twentieth century Black culture, sharing multiple allusions to sociopolitical and cultural events, the workings of daily speech, references to what is often marginalized. Because quiltmaking is often Mullen's metaphor, the quatrains appear as quilt squares of polyphonic sound, as fabric made of music. Careening through meaning and meanings, with its incessant punning, secret jokes, and half-phrases, the poem makes a playful *logopoeia* from idiomatic shorthand, nonrepresentational and representational language that is endlessly inventive. In other contexts, literary clichés might be deadening, but Mullen's field of received phrases forms a flexible linguistic commons, energizing the reader with its dynamic playfulness, nuanced references, and riddles. Mullen repurposes the phrase "a crime against the state" to give it fresh relevance, and the quilt and fabric metaphors are made from music—"knots mend the string quilt / of kente stripped when kin split // white covers of black material / dense fabric that obeys its own logic"—so

that the quilt forms its own order. Students often ob-
serve that Mullen's poem is antihierarchical; not only
does it allow the tonal shifts and sounds of collective
speakers, at times a single speaker or ancestral voices
break through with micro-choruses. When I first read
this book, I felt breathless with its energy and force. I
was grateful to Mullen for being among the poetic sis-
ters who created bridges instead of borders, for easing
a perceived tension between poetry of abstract materi-
ality and that of lyric representation. *Muse and Drudge*
resists the easy take and rewards rereading, drawing to-
gether music, meaning, and mystery in a "Song of Her-
selves." It is a truly great work of art.

| | | | \ | | | | | | \ | ) \ |

At times, choosing an atypical technique might have
deep implication for an artist. A few years ago, Brian
Teare presented a brilliant talk about reading lyric po-
etry at a conference just after the massacre of forty-nine
people at a predominantly gay Latinx nightclub in Or-
lando, Florida. Teare discussed *Bright Felon* by Kazim
Ali, a book-length prose poem with a complex narra-
tive about Ali's experience of coming out as a gay man
in a Muslim family. Teare summarized what is urgent
about some kinds of lyric complexity, noting, *"Bright*

*Felon* tells the story of the crucial role poetry and lyric language play in Ali's turn away from destructive self-hatred toward survival and self-knowledge: 'Only through art, not my own body, could I keep myself breathing.'" Teare noted that Ali's poem resists the easy devices of a "successful coming out" story in favor of a complexly imbricated sentence structure, collaged and layered, as the necessary way the poet had of conveying the complexity of his experience and literally of saving his own life. Teare invoked the poet-philosopher Jan Zwicky's term "lyric thinking" for nonlinearity, shifts, and paradoxes, to invoke the meaning of an experience. The self-contradictory style was essential to free the poet from paralysis, and Teare pointed to the way in which some difficulty and contradiction might be far more true than common truisms.

| | | | \ | | | | | ) | \ | \ |

As inner meditations and hypnotherapy have accompanied my journey in poetry, there seem many more doorways. Through attention we engage with what is seemingly incompatible, just as my local plum tree is both natural and symbolic, on a beautiful but endangered earth, a full expression of nonhuman nature. My beloved teacher Charles Wright once told me about the

Bride tree

seer called Pseudo-Dionysus, a visionary Syrian prophet
from the sixth century who wrote texts with titles like
"What is the Divine Gloom?" that recommend engage-
ment with the "super-luminous gloom of silence" that
is "altogether impalpable and invisible"; later, the work
of the German mystic Jakob Boehme brought together

Kabbalistic and Gnostic notions of mystical unity. The early Gnostics, not always at ease with the material world, used inner knowledge as a source. Such visionary and prophetic traditions accentuated a perceived "split" in nature, between what we experience with our senses and the mysteries beyond the senses, might not be necessarily dualistic but a dialectical exchange of energies. One can be of two minds about being dualist. The intuition techniques I devised out of my hypnotherapy were mostly quite practical and writing-oriented. Here is part of the process: Setting aside an hour, I would close my eyes and draw an inner circle. The first emanations were often not understandable. But later, in dialogue with the images of the circle, the toxic thought or condition or figure might become less so, and the intuition would come. Throughout my life I've spoken to plants, animals, and inanimate things to bridge the great divide between the visible and the invisible worlds, and although many of my spiritual practices exist on several levels and address the houseplants, I do not believe the plants share my feelings.

| | | | \ | | | | | ) | \ | \ |

I have three more poems of meaning and mystery. This is by the Chuvash poet Gennady Aygi.

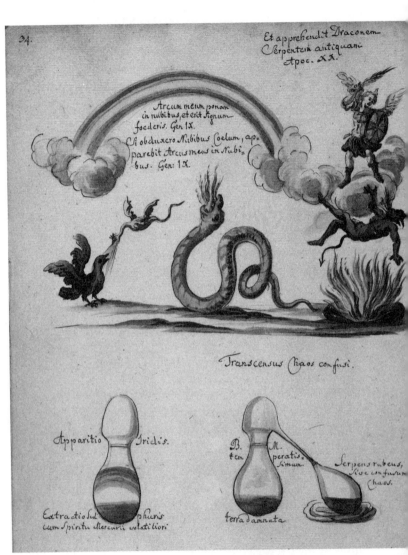

Illustration from *Thesaurus thesaurorum*, c. 17

## Field: In the Full Blaze of Winter

*To René Char*

god-pyre!—this open field
letting all things pass through (mile-posts and wind and distant

specks of mills: all more and more—as if from this

world—not waking—gathering distance: oh all these

are sparks—not rending the flame of the pyre-that-is-

not-of-this-universe)
"I am"—without trace of anything whatever
not-of-this-universe shining
god-pyre

Peter France's translation renders Aygi's work so beau-
tifully that I almost don't feel deprived not reading
Russian, and he creates a syntactic precarity like a del-
icately strung net. This poem brings together the met-
aphor and metonymy we spoke of last week, though
the image does not say overtly that the fire "stands
for" anything; rather, it is in the same place as the di-
vine. It is a poem about someone observing a field in
winter and having an ecstatic experience through lan-
guage, and it is in the nature of Aygi's poetry to make
simple images that are unutterably mysterious. At the
level of poetic craft, this poem demonstrates epana-
lepsis, as the neologism and concept of the "god-pyre"

occurs at both the beginning and the end of the piece, which in itself brings a dancing circularity of the god figure. Enveloped in phrases that are simultaneously full and empty, the poet wants to be outside of language, to be transported, and almost is, but it is impossible to be outside of language and still make an utterance. The mystical transcendence in Aygi's open form shines through its visual devices. The image of a flame in an open field, in winter, in fragments like sparks, is very a Gnostic and Kabbalistic image, in which the word/logos occupies the force of god-spirit. The poem burns through and consumes its own images, just as the observing presence of the poet-self is consumed by the process of observing; a Hopkinsian self-interruption of "oh all these are sparks" seems to burn the ego of the observer as well. A seamless or continuous syntax would not create this effect; Aygi's broken form allows the meaning to rush through in partial sentences with kinetic energy and light. The presence of many em-dashes and hyphens acts as visual kindling for the pyre; there is no pure flame without being here, speaking about it, and yet only by stripping down the language can the poet arrive in consciousness. Celan's influence can be felt in the breathtaking bursts of images; Emily Dickinson can be felt in the punctuation. The poet's vision is seen as an extension of light and heat.

| | | | \ | | | | | ) | \ | \ |

Here is a Dickinson piece, written a century before Aygi's poem, one that also deploys an image of ignition. Many of Emily Dickinson's poems derive from internal energetic collisions.

The Zeroes taught us—Phosphorous
We learned to like the Fire
By playing Glaciers—when a Boy
And Tinder—guessed—by power
Of opposite—to balance Odd
If white—a Red—must be
Paralysis—our Primer—dumb
Unto Vitality!

Fire and ice are presented not as dueling forces but as figures for a process of experiential learning. Dickinson proposes an evocative paradox with a series of protracted or deferred meanings about the way certain learning occurs; knowledge happens through recognizing contradiction. We start from the Zeroes (the naught) where we are already on the floor of ourselves, a spiritual state of nothingness. Phosphorous produces a very great bright light, a mini-explosion like inspiration. As a historical note, safety matches, equipped with phosphorous, first became widely available in 1844.

Dickinson would have been fourteen years old. The phosphorous, a highly flammable agent, was concentrated at the tip, in white or yellow; a household match could, for the first time, ignite from "zero" to flame with a single strike. Women working in the match factories were some of the most vulnerable factory workers in the nineteenth century; handling the phosphorous caused loss of bone and crippling disability. Annie Besant, the theosophist, advocated for the Match Girls in their rebellion later in the century and provided a model for me for activist practice that includes spiritually radical beliefs.

"We learned to like the fire / By playing Glaciers . . ." —we can only learn to endure intense experiences by knowing their perceived opposites. "When a Boy . . ."—Dickinson is of her time; she knows that holding power is available to "a Boy," and she calls forth a male figure or persona to represent her anima. In lines 4–5, the sentence divides: "Tinder" goes grammatically either with the previous line or with "to balance Odd," and we allow for a pun on *tinder/tender*. Dickinson reminds us that we learn through paradox, to balance things by being unbalanced and experiencing opposites, but that these apparent paradoxes, including the white and red of the struck match, make for fire/insight/ sight; she even notes that what we experience as paralysis might be a sort of first instruction, a primer, for learning how to have agency, to reconcile what cannot be reconciled. I feel close to this deeply compressed, strange poem. Some think Dickinson's long strokes conduct and caress the silences, interrupt the force of grammar; some think they are purely visual; some think they are sonorous elocutionary marks, stresses for emphasis. Their meaning is in their mystery.

Sometimes when I read Dickinson, I'm reminded of a secret script called Nüshu script, invented in the last few centuries in the mountains of China in the Jiangyong region. The script was devised by women so they could write only to each other. The characters, long and elegant, were a kind of code. The gender specific script was used for passing encoded messages across communities. There are only a few Nüshu writers left, but the script survives; there are about 720 characters used in songs, prayers, embroidery. When I look at this script, I think of how the mystery at the heart of things fills us with existential hope. The delicate and elegant signs look like organic creatures—beaks, stems, little stands—with an intense secrecy held between the ragged columns.

| | | | | \ | \ | | | | | ) \ |

The last poem for tonight is Robert Duncan's "Often I am Permitted to Return to a Meadow," a much-loved poem that builds meaning in spite of—and because of—a spiraling syntax.

### Often I Am Permitted to Return to a Meadow

as if it were a scene made-up by the mind,
that is not mine, but is a made place,

that is mine, it is so near to the heart,
an eternal pasture folded in all thought
so that there is a hall therein

that is a made place, created by light
wherefrom the shadows that are forms fall.

Wherefrom fall all architectures I am
I say are likenesses of the First Beloved
whose flowers are flames lit to the Lady.

She it is Queen Under The Hill
whose hosts are a disturbance of words within words
that is a field folded.

It is only a dream of the grass blowing
east against the source of the sun
in an hour before the sun's going down

whose secret we see in a children's game
of ring a round of roses told.

Often I am permitted to return to a meadow
as if it were a given property of the mind
that certain bounds hold against chaos,

that is a place of first permission,
everlasting omen of what is.

The fuguelike lines, the mythic imagery and music—
"that is not mine . . . that is mine . . . that is a made
place . . . that is a made place"—tumble together. The
legible title slyly gives us a sense that we can paraphrase
this poem: "Often I (the poet or the reader) travel to
a place in my mind that gives me a sense of freedom
and permission; there I (or we) have a relationship to
an interior, imaginative, symbolic realm and with fa-
miliar figures (the First Beloved, the Queen Under the
Hill) who also remind me (or us) or the first language,
children at play; and this place to which I can return
gives a sense of internal order and feels to me timeless."
But a paraphrase of a poem is not the poem, and we
risk making it sound too easy. The poem's connotative
power is gained only through the exact clusters of ab-
stract phrasings: "Wherefrom fall all architectures I
am / I say are likenesses of the First Beloved / whose
flowers are flames lit to the Lady." And the mysteries re-
main. "Often I am permitted"—lures us in the passive
voice—I don't do the permitting, I *am permitted*—to

return to a meadow. Which meadow? It's not in Yosemite or in Switzerland. "As if it were a scene made-up by the mind"—if my mind is making the meadow, why must I receive the permission? Then the enfolded: "that is not mine, but is a made place, // that is mine, it is so near to the heart, / an eternal pasture folded in all thought." This place is made by my mind, but I don't own it? And it is near to the heart yet it is eternal and folded everywhere: "there is a hall therein // that is a made place, created by light / wherefrom the shadows that are forms fall." We are taken through a place that is both a meadow and a hallway and is neither, in folded syntax, just as the Pacific plate buckles under the main continent near where Duncan lived in San Francisco. By now we see this meadow is not so much a place as it is a process. With all of its mystery, this poem holds out against the desire to take an easy route.

| | | | \ | | | \ | | | | ) \ |

In closing, I hope these examples and stories help you to try new things and to be less afraid of not instantly understanding. I began this talk in April 2020 and I'm putting the finishing touches on it during Trump's second impeachment. Over our heads, geese honk, heading somewhere, channeling random energy

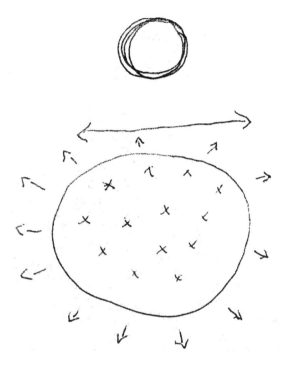

"Brenda's idea of time," pencil drawing, author's notebook

and rare motion into their Edwardian script of a V. California geese seem not to have a clue when to migrate, but I know their instincts have greater force than my limited vision.

Next week I will speak on Magic and Morality, with some thoughts about political poetry and activist poetics. Your homework for this week is to close your eyes and imagine a circle populated with a figure you are in dialogue with in calm moments. I asked a philosopher friend to do this and he said he was going to try it with Wittgenstein. I give you permission to be strange, to bring together in your reading and writing what you encounter in your inner world. Many of your tools to engage with the unknown are already inside you. Here is a picture of time I drew in my notebook.

We need healthcare and the vaccine, we need housing and food, an end to racism and wars. We also need art that brings news from the larger symbolic sphere where the worlds of myth and poetry connect us to other humans, to individual, cultural, and national histories, as well as to the planet of nonhuman creatures. The great writer Audre Lorde reminds us that poetry is not a luxury. Dreams are also not luxuries and are necessary mysteries. Poetry is part of our collective dream realm, and it returns to the collective. Joseph dreamed his people would be spared from the plague. A colleague told me she had her "first social distancing dream" in which everyone was masked. How does meaning occur when we are interpreting anything? The daily miracle of making meaning occurs trillions of times in brains of *homo sapiens* on earth each second as humans try to parse not just what words signify in thousands of languages but also what they mean in terms of the vastness of lived experience. Like an ancient alchemist, when you turn to poetry or any art, you are still trying to figure out the third side in the triangle of mystery and meaning, which only you can provide.

# MAGIC
*and*
# MORALITY

Every morning I wake up and talk to my orchids. They're named after French poets: Baudelaire, Rimbaud, Verlaine, Mallarmé, Apollinaire, Bréton. Sordello is a recent acquisition. A previous Rimbaud died because I overwatered him, but the others are doing well; Mallarmé and Verlaine have put up new spikes, though Mallarmé has a suspicious yellow leaf. John Ruskin warned poets against the pathetic fallacy, the practice of injecting false or excessive feeling into nonhuman nature. My naming the plants is a form of friendliness. Do the orchids hear my morning greeting? No. Do I believe the orchids have experiences? Depends on what an "experience" is, but theirs is not mine; they have orchid experiences. Are my orchids inspirited? Yes, if the idea of spirit can be a loose metaphorical concept that shows respect.

Orchids in Brenda Hillman's home 2021

The title of tonight's talk is "Magic and Morality." I will share examples of poems with moral force, will speak about some justice activist work I've done, and will try to relate it to writing and reading practices in ways that I hope will be of use. When I conceived of these three talks as a toolkit for a functional imagination in times of crisis, I suspected this third topic might require the largest stretch; Magic seems far from Morality. But I hope if you've attended either of the previous lectures—Metaphor and Metonymy, Meaning and Mystery—you'll see some connections.

| | | | \ | | | | | \ | | ) \ |

What is called a moral life—living according to a set of values that might lead to a greater good—is not considered a specialty of poets. Poets like to misbehave and so do our dream lives. The anarchist tendencies of my own imagination are often in conflict with my ethical values. Even great political poems—Blake's "London," Ginsberg's "Howl," Audre Lorde's "Power"—that stake out moral claims clearly sometimes express conflicting emotional registers. Human communities assemble institutions and systems based on rational laws, but symbolic worlds of art and myth often begin with uncertainty, turbulent emotion, and ungovernable impulses. For Plato, poets don't even belong in the Republic because we are liars and renegades. Poets mostly don't specialize in adulthood, though we can do convincing adult imitations such as reading warning labels on food, stopping at traffic signals, occasionally apologizing to our loved ones for our malfeasance. My own creative

Justice vigil at Saint Mary's College

life is lawless, with magical concepts woven into days that seem laden with too much anxious responsibility, so my odd thinking needs to be tucked away and I juggle opposing models of reality. In a vigil I organized at my place of work for fifteen years, I had secret conversations with oaks, lichens, beetles, and mosses, as well as with the souls of dead writers who joined our vigil. I named my introverted practice "crypto-animist activism," a term that appears in a fascinating book edited by Linda Russo and Marthe Reed called *Counter-Desecration: A Glossary of terms for Writing in the Anthropocene.* As I noted in my second talk, we are shrouded in mystery: the universe is 68 percent dark energy, 27 percent dark matter, so by my poet's math, we know 95 percent of nothing about anything. It's hard to understand how humans became so arrogant.

Tonight I will begin with some very short poems of moral vision. I chose these brief exquisite works—written in five lines, two lines, two lines, one line, and nine lines respectively—to demonstrate how powerfully poetry can present complex moral issues in compact spaces. They are short pieces, so most of my commentaries will be brief notes on their craft. Let's start with an iconic piece by Randall Jarrell.

### Death of a Ball Turret Gunner

From my mother's sleep I fell into the State,
And I hunched in its belly till my wet fur froze.
Six miles from earth, loosed from its dream of life,
I woke to black flak and the nightmare fighters.
When I died they washed me out of the turret with a hose.

Spoken in the posthumous "voice" of a young airman killed in action in WWII, written in accentual five-stress lines until the last line, this is one of the great antiwar poems. "From my mother's sleep I fell into the State." To be a soldier for the State—capital *S,* but with lowercase "state" intended—is to fall precipitously from nonbirth into nonbirth. Only in line 4 is the young solder briefly awake to life—black flak, nightmare fighters. The image of the gunner falling from mother's womb to the unborn state of the war, a furry fetal presence, always evinces a deep grief in my students when they understand the way its compressed power allows them to register how in five lines it makes a case against war, as the unborn soldier vanishes in the coffin-womb of history where gestation and birth are coterminous with death.

| | | | \ | | | \ | | | | ) \ |

"Brevity" by Camille Dungy, deploys one grammatical fragment of twelve words.

Brevity

As in four girls; Sunday
dresses: bone, ash, ash, bone, ash, bone.

Brevity, the title, is of course tautological. This is an homage to Addie Mae Collins, Cynthia Wesley, Carole Robertson, and Carol Denise McNair who died in the Birmingham 16th Street Baptist Church bombing on September 15, 1963. With flawless precision, Dungy summons the memory of four girls in two lines with three units of perception. It is a micro-sonata of memory, an elegy and a poem of moral outrage—six words, two words repeated three times after a colon:

"bone, ash, ash, bone, ash, bone." The poet uses a single moment of inversion to achieve surprising power; the expected order of the words would of course have been "bone, ash, bone, ash, bone, ash," but in Dungy's order, the word "ash" is framed by the word "bone," rendering the physical fate of the children in a heartbreaking, un-expected reversal. The rhetorical device is epizeuxis—a word repeated in quick succession. The poem's trans-formative authority omits all excess; it seems to allow an implied space for a different outcome.

| | | | \ | | | | | | \ | ) \ |

Another two-line poem, this one by Korean poet Kim Hyesoon, brilliantly translated by Don Mee Choi.

Already

*Day twenty-eight*

You are already born inside death
(echoes 49 times)

Kim Hyesoon's *Autobiography of Death* is a sociopolit-ical history of violence by means of forty-nine linked shamanic and allegorical poems, with illustrations by the artist Fi Jae Li. Each poem is an entry in a notebook Death has kept throughout Korea's turbulent past, each an ironic slice of tonal magic. Images of Death's "life" mutate endlessly, emerging and retreating dramatically, empowered in their journey by various devices of repetition. Death's notebook entry here is a one-line poem attached to a weightily specific and almost cumbersome numerical note, for a total of two lines. The parenthetical note states that the personified death will be echoed forty-nine times, creating the sense that an individual destiny will always be overwhelmed by the endless and cumulative power of death and silenced by space. What creates such a brief poem's magical force? The personified death-parent gestates the life force, and noting this repetition in advance produces an arbitrarily bitter and surreal wit. The book-length sequence is saturated with profound color and energy even as the entry for each "day" presents a catastrophe of history and a consolidated fate brought about by Korea's boundless suffering through war.

| | | | \ | | | | | | \ | ) \ |

Here is another very short poem, this one by Arthur Sze, whose book *Sight Lines* has a group of single-lined, untitled poems that depict collisions between the natural beauty of New Mexico and the weapons industry in that region.

—A man who built plutonium triggers breeds horses now—

Small poems with this kind of power are in themselves nuclear reactors. Sze's riveting singlets are scattered through the book as stand-alone poems and also form a continuous poem with the force of a single brush stroke. Some of the poems are set off by dashes, as is this one, as if to stretch it to its own margins. This one is a kind of ambulatory, stretched alexandrine, with seven stresses. In the middle of the line, the dire phrase "plutonium trigger"—four syllables then two—is abstractly graceful even as it describes a weapon unleashing meaningless terror on the voiceless landscape that has horses—and not just any horses, carefully bred horses. The line is a poem with moral weight; it enacts a world in which the maker of compressed explosives also makes new animals, and the reader must accept that fact; it suggests that creation in and of itself is raw energy, not necessarily friendly and not necessarily in service of moral outcomes. It is a wise and baffling image-line-scene about the power of humans to create a world by manipulating nature. It leaves us a bit confused and uncertain. How are we supposed to feel? Should we enjoy the irony of human engagement to make matter more violent then more beautiful? This is the opposite of a preachy or polemical speech.

| | | | \ | | | | | ) | \ | \ |

Bob Hass's *Little Book on Form* offers satire as one of the four categories of poetry and includes most political poetry in that designation. He notes that the word *satire* comes from "satura"—a Latin word for a mixed fruit stew. Listen to the satiric tonal mix in a nine-line, twenty-one word poem by Amiri Baraka.

### Monday in B-Flat

I can pray
     all day
     & God
     wont come.

But if I call
     911
     The Devil
      be here

     in a minute!

The piece is effective in part because of the collision of tones, definitely a *satura* or mixed stew in which contradictory effects are brought together. It is a wiry poem: 3-2-2-2 4-1-2-2-3 words per line; the first two lines have an end-rhyme. It presents at first as a sort of joke because the slightly self-effacing speaker "I" remarks casually in two short sentences about the futility of prayer. But the joke quality is short-lived; the second sentence turns bitterly satirical, a single metaphor equating state law enforcement with the Devil—not a lowercase devil, Satan himself, and the history of state violence against Black people is in evidence. Like our other examples, its main feature is an exemplary compression. I need hardly say that this poem has lost none of its relevance.

I hope these five dynamic examples demonstrate how powerfully poetry can communicate a visionary force without declamatory speeches, sometimes using only a few lines, sometimes only one.

| | | | \ | | | | | ) | \ | \ |

I'm sometimes called a "poet-activist" but that is inaccurate; activists are dynamic and idealistic, often with outgoing personalities. I am an anxious introvert. Like many of my generation, I was politically active in the late sixties and seventies; the activities I will describe tonight began after the post-911 invasion of Afghanistan and Iraq, when my disgust over US imperialism, continuing horror at racial inequality, and mounting anxiety about climate reached new levels. Few people my age were taking action outside their comfort zones, even as people of color and whites in the working classes experienced widening economic disparity. Friends on the far left waited for the revolution and engaged in gloomy conversations. After the US invaded Iraq, I fell into a profound depression. When Bob and I were visiting Berlin, I had a somatic experience standing in a courtyard near a train stop where Jews were carried to Auschwitz. I felt the eyes of apartment dwellers peering down from their windows, piercing my body with painful light rays. When Bob and I got back to the US I decided to become more politically engaged, including doing war tax resistance.

Kensington, CA 94708
July 18, 2005

Internal Revenue Service
Odgen, UT 84201-0030

Dear Internal Revenue Service:

Thank you for your letter number xxxx regarding my 2004 Federal Tax Return. As I indicated in my letters of March 10 and April 18, 2005, my taxes were prepared to the full extent of the law. I enclosed a check for $xxxx, the taxes owed for 2004, minus $xxxx. I understand that the amount owed is $xxxx as of this writing.

I will continue to withhold this amount in protest against the ongoing war in Iraq. One-sixth of every tax dollar is going to the war; therefore, I am withholding one-sixth of my taxes due. I spoke to an employee #xxxx in your office who verified that all my employment information is correct. She mentioned that if I would like to protest the war in Iraq, I should talk to my congressional representatives about ways to protest within the law. As far as I can tell, my congressional representatives are powerless to fight the current policies, or they no longer care to insist on an exit strategy.

I cannot continue to pay for a war based on false premises. Our government has admitted that there were no weapons of mass destruction in Iraq, the premise upon which the war was waged. Many lives continue to be lost and there is no exit strategy planned. Ordinary citizens must make some protest against this needless war and not continue to accept the current operations.

The IRS employee I spoke to indicated it would be necessary to contact my employer to extract the amount from my salary or directly from my bank account. I understand that this will be happening and the reasons.

Because I am a teacher in California, I sincerely hope that the rest of my tax dollars will go to improved education, social services, and healthcare for the adults and children in our cities and countryside. That should be what American government is all about.

Sincerely,
Brenda Hillman

taxpayer #xxxxxxxxxx

Antiwar protest at the Heritage Foundation, 2007

Tax resistance is not what it was in the days of Thoreau; you can fight the computers for several years, but then they simply attach your wages. It is nearly impossible to go to jail for not paying war taxes. I began to work with CodePink, a grassroots group of women activists. Our first campaign was to lobby state legislators to pass AJR36, a resolution to bring National Guard troops home from Iraq. I privately committed to doing actions that could have a poetic or spiritual component, that could use my writing skills. After visiting a state assemblymember's office one rainy day, seeing many washed up earthworms on the capitol steps, I visualized new laws being written in a language of worms. In the years that followed, our group traveled frequently to DC to protest the wars and to lobby. Our goal was show up in our bodies as women in so-called zones of power. I took red-eye flights so I could visit offices on Fridays without missing class. Some women in our group had given up jobs and had left loved ones to do this grass-roots justice work. Many were risking multiple arrests and doing jail time. Many were mothers and grand-mothers, teachers and working-class women. We at-tended congressional hearings, organized, phoned, and faxed; we did sit-ins and die-ins, did civil disobedience, sang in the Capitol rotunda, did many street theater actions.

In one action, we showed up at the Department of Justice for the federal trial of Scooter Libby, George W. Bush's scoundrel assistant, and we were told that we couldn't go in wearing pink shirts, so took off our shirts and stood outside until they let us in. The Constitution doesn't state you cannot wear pink. At the Democratic convention in Denver, Janet Weil and I read poetry in the "free speech cage" (it was called the free speech area, but it was a very large cage) to a group of cops who were guarding us in the cage. It was quite a scene: two women reading poetry in a cage, six police officers watching and laughing. I was often confused about how

Heron at the Capitol, 2007

to be a poet during those years but I took my notebook and sometimes drafted lines during congressional hearings or other government settings; on the grounds of official spaces, I read notes to nonhuman creatures. One afternoon, I interviewed dead bugs on the Capitol carpet. In a Senate committee chamber, there was a fly buzzing around the room and I thought of the Babylonian goddess Ishtar. I tried to include nonhuman creatures, so the fly could be included in a poem, not just the data about the arms sales. The names of the Congressional bills merged with nonhuman species and the endangered life forms of the Anacostia River watershed

Rayburn building display of military equipment, 2007

near the Capitol, the mosses and lichens clinging to buildings, the fungal spots on plants in the offices.

From these times, it was obvious many mental layers can be included in political actions. In Lafayette Park, poems could be whispered to the air and to rocks, remembering the history of the land and those to whom it belonged. I was horrified about some of what I learned in the mid-aughts; the munitions manufacturers had their "war wares" set up right across the hall from where congressional hearings were occurring.

Across from one congressional hearing room where they discussed costly military garb called Dragonskin to be used for desert warfare, there was a large display of semiautomatic weapons. Our group of women began to sing across from the guns until they led us out. To record the sales of Dragonskin outfits, I was tapping in the hearing room on my paper, using punctuation as a form of comfort music. From the rooftop of the Federal Reserve, I imagined shrinking, colorful numbers flying toward the Midwest. During a protest at the Heritage Foundation, a right wing think tank, a staff person took my camera and smashed my head; I grabbed it back and saved the photo card.

I have thought often about what the job of a poet is now. You can take poetry and poetic actions to official spaces and it is not a frivolous activity. Janet and I took antiwar poems to our representative's chief of staff and asked if we could read to her; she listened and we spoke about the poems we had brought. I told my congressman if he didn't stop voting for the war funding, he would end up being named in my poem for eternity. I

was surprised when his staff person called our adminis-
trative assistant at Saint Mary's and asked her to tell me
he had voted against the war funding.

| | | | \ | | | | | ) | \ | \ |

I no longer travel to DC to protest or talk to repre-
sentatives face to face; the carbon footprint is too great.
But I learned a great deal about the legislative process,
how to negotiate with elected officials. I learned many
laws are made by young staffers who don't take lunch
breaks. They do the real work, keeping track of how the
votes go on any issue. Learning their names and keeping
the names of the bills in your mind is key. I learned that
most legislators focus on the powerful lobbyists, but in-
dividuals have power to meet and act and bring imag-
inative language. I learned the value of different kinds
of discourse in political poems, that one can mix data
and magic to include several models of reality. Once at
a die-in, I thought, maybe this is the opposite of poetry.
Then I thought, no, poetic space and the political space
are not two different spaces. Poetry is not a decoration,
to be used just for weddings and funerals.

When I began putting documents in poems in my
books on the elements, not many contemporaries were
doing that so I looked to models from the past: to Muriel

Rukeyser's poetry, to Theresa Hak Kyung Cha's *Dictée*, to Denise Levertov's antiwar hybrid poems. After the fly incident in Washington, I realized that bringing names and documents into poems could augment the enterprise. Emerging poets, please don't forget those who have cut paths for you to navigate seemingly incompatible truths, and if you don't find models for what you want to do, make them yourself. In the early 2000s, there were not as many poet activists as there are now. It was frowned upon by some when I started. The most important thing is to write what you want to read and to do it with heart.

|   |   |   |   |   \   |   |   |   |   |   |   \   |   )   \   |

Many quiet poems of moral vision may not seem political but can make intense statements with laser effects. Here's a poem by Tomas Tranströmer, translated by Robert Bly, that offers a critique of bourgeois life with no moral bromides or pronouncements.

### Below Freezing

We are at a party that doesn't love us. Finally the party lets the mask fall and shows what it is: a shunting station for freight cars. In the fog cold giants stand on their tracks. A scribble of chalk on the car doors.

    One can't say it aloud, but there is a lot of repressed violence here. That is why the furnishings seem so heavy. And why it is so difficult to see the other thing present: a spot of sun that moves over the house walls and slips over the unaware forest of flickering faces, a biblical saying never set down: "Come unto me, for I am as full of contradictions as you."

I work the next morning in a different town. I drive there in a hum through the dawning hour that resembles a blue cylinder. Orion hangs over the frost. Children stand in a silent clump, waiting for the school bus, the children no one prays for. The light grows as gradually as our hair.

I think of this poem frequently when I'm at a dull social gathering: "We are at a party that doesn't love us"; "there is a lot of repressed violence here." The furnishings of the interior setting are heavy, as if absorbing a mood of spiritual torpor, and they take on the weight of lead. A party of loveless adults in a zone of existential heaviness seems like something out of a Bergman film, and this place of unrealized middle-class suffering with its strange cosmic sunspot passing over it connects to a scene of solitary children at the bus stop, which we see through the perspective of a morning commuter. When I see children in clumps in California, looking solitary, I think of the line, "the children no one prays for." The poet introduces a note of profound empathy, a strange calm beauty and otherness, with the image of the blue cylinder that seems to emerge from the mind of the commuting observer. An almost magical property is introduced as the reader tracks the consciousness of detached observation, along with the suggestion of moral querulousness. This is not a poem that conforms to any category of "political poetry," yet the poet critiques a scene of bourgeois life with feeling and depth.

| | | | | \ | \ | | | | | | ) | \ |

Here is a piece by Paul Celan, brilliantly translated by Ben Friedlander. I keep this poem near my desk at all times.

Eternity decays: in
Cerveteri the
asphodels
ask each other white.

With mumbling ladles
out of death-kettle,
over stone, over stone,
they spoon soup
in every bed
and camp.

The power of this poem begins in the first two dramatic words: Eternity decays. Cerveteri in Italy is the site of many tombs from the Etruscan period; in the first stanza we see white flowers (asphodels were for William Carlos Williams a flower with great energy) growing on tombs and Eternity decaying. Recent correspondence with Ben Friedlander illuminates his choices; he writes: "The German is 'Die Ewigkeit altert'; 'Ages' or 'gets old' would be more literal but the reference to Cerveteri nudged me toward decay." In the second stanza, the surreal symbolic "death-kettle" is set in an ominous six-line scene that alludes to death camps." This eerie, mystical poem depicts the history of the Holocaust collapsed in the image of a "death-kettle" time when even eternity will end. In Friedlander's breathtaking English rendering, "ladle" and "kettle" rhyme. The demotic, the temporal and the eternal are collapsed together in a few lines. As in the short poems I discussed earlier, compression is the key. Huge transformations of historical moments can occur in a few images. In political action, you have to be receptive and you have to let go of outcomes. That principle stays with me as a poetics statement too. Celan, like Dickinson, often writes most powerfully from a sense of powerlessness and precarity, and heads straight into the paradox. In these moments poetry seems to retain an impossible strength, and it has everything to offer a culture that fattens itself on retaliatory violence.

|  |  |  |  |  \  |  \  |  |  |  |  |  |  )  \  |

Protestors at Occupy Cal

I want to talk a bit about risk-taking in poems of social conscience, about keeping categories loose, about operating in uncertainty and process, and questioning subjectivity and ego in ways that will enhance subtlety.

These things of course apply in political processes and in human negotiations as well as in poetry. I still have much to learn about this. Life is very large, and there's no such thing as the not-poem. Every bit of it can go with poetry. Community organizers might seem to be different from poets in that they see language as a tool for getting messages across. Practicing speaking to media, we did many "soundbite" exercises, in case a reporter came and said, "What brings you out here today?" Besides, the poems chosen for rallies and political events sometimes deploy obvious rhetorical strategies or are insistently declamatory. When I tried to introduce my activist friends to innovative poetry I love, at first they did not get it. The word "siloed" comes to mind. Modernist poetry is siloed, and political organizing is siloed. Microsoft has put a little red squiggle under "siloed." It asks if I prefer "silex."

I used to think you couldn't read subtle or spiritual poetry at a political rally, but in fact, you can bring all kinds of poetry anywhere. Poets need not conform to the preachy or the polemical. A group of us protested with Occupy in West Oakland while reading Robert Duncan's "Poem Beginning with a Line by Pindar," passing the poem back and forth. It is the same with stretching your imagination about beings that are there, beings that were there before you, showing respect for

Police in riot gear at Occupy Oakland

the foxes that are in the hills, not far away. In one city block there are thousands of miles of spider webs; each orb-weaver spider has eight eyes. Later that month at Occupy Cal, Bob and I had a less friendly meeting with

Berkeley law enforcement when we opposed the re-
moval of tents on campus and I somehow caught sight
of a row of ants going about their business on a wall
during this brutal encounter. The row of ants went into
my poem and so did a long rift down the page.

Uncertainty is a quality poets and community ac-
tivists share—uncertainty about outcomes, to abide
in doubt, to accommodate both process thinking and
disappointment. Neither poets nor activists know what
will happen at the end of a particular composition or
action. Uncertainty is crucial to the poetic process and
to political organizing. Activism is not like flossing;
you don't have to reach every tooth and pre-imagined
outcomes can be given up. A poet's power derives
from powerlessness, traveling straight into the paradox
where poems are impossible utterances.

One winter, Bob and I met Janet Weil and Kat Factor
at Creech Air Force Base in Nevada, where they fly the
predator drones; we did a vigil for a few days, reading
poetry outside the base as the enlisted folks drove in.
Police came by and showed us the line we couldn't cross.
As we were being observed and as eyeless drones flew
very close overhead, I tried imagining, as Joni Mitchell
writes in "Woodstock," that the drones turned into but-
terflies, or at least wasps with dangly legs; we flattened
our books and held them up for the drone to photo-

Janet Weil at Creech Air Force Base

graph, imagining young pilots flying the drones inside the base in their shorts, looking at a poem instead of practicing to kill someone at a wedding in Yemen. This became part of the process.

I spoke last week about the use of trance or the waking dream; this can be useful during stressful actions. Behaving unconventionally like this may seem embarrassing, but using robots to bomb helpless people half a world away is intolerable.

Several years ago, some graduate students and I organized Prophets not Profits and traveled nearby to read poems near the sites of local oil refineries. We in-

Poetry reading at the entrance to Creech

voked a figure from ceremonial Celtic ritual, the Angel
of the Third Altitude, a childlike figure of innocence
dressed with bay and laurel leaves, and because it was
Halloween we wore costumes. Some poets went into

the refinery office to ask if we could read poems to the staff; the staff, not surprisingly, said no, and sent a white truck to follow us to make sure we weren't violent. As we read poems facing the giant vats at the refineries at Valero and Chevron, one poet who had worked for many years in the petroleum industry, Ross Belot, told us a story about the bacteria that are used in the refining process, and as we faced the containers, I thought of the tiny beings, wondering what their experience is like, and how they belong in poetry. Would those in the white trucks develop alternative energy sources, to save the wildlife destroyed by the process of extraction? Poets are always vulnerable, and when standing outside with their poems, even more so.

A few months later, after Trump started to dismantle environmental protections, we took a similar action to a suburban shopping center, but this time we wore Russian gas masks we had purchased on the internet. Here is an account I wrote in my notebook: *Grassy hills with their so-called invasive species surrounded us. After we began our action a man came up to us & asked what we were doing. I said we were reading ecological poetry outdoors as part of a class because the EPA was in trouble. He said he owned the Safeway & we would have to take our protest elsewhere. I thought of the gas tank of his Volvo full of screaming dead animals from the Cre-*

Oil refinery protest, Halloween 2015

taceous, a 40 million year geologic period of "shallow inland seas," a phrase I've always found comforting. We moved our action to a different spot and continued reading. The rubber tubes of our gas masks, used perhaps in the Soviet era, looked like snouts of ancient anteaters dangling down over the pages or our phones. At first it was hard to see the poems through the scratched eye goggles, & then we got the hang of it. I wondered what happened to our interlocutor; how he would live out his days, without poetry?

During the Obama years, Bob and I were invited to come to DC to protest the Keystone Pipeline with a

Reading poetry in Russian gas masks at
an environmental protest

couple of prominent environmental groups. It was the
first time the Sierra Club proposed civil disobedience,
to bring awareness at a time when Obama was wavering
under pressure from the fossil fuel industry about going
ahead with the pipeline. Some blocked passage on the
sidewalks, which is a misdemeanor; others chained
themselves to the White House fence. There was a
priest available because it was Ash Wednesday. Capitol
Hill police put us into police vans and took us to the

Reading more poetry in gas masks

station in Maryland to be booked. When the young cop was writing up my arrest, he asked if I had tattoos or identifying marks. I described my two tattoos for him. The officer and I were both white, but I felt the chasm of class difference widen when I couldn't ask him about his own tattoo.

| | | | \ | | | | | | \ | ) \ |

To close my series of lectures, I'd like to talk about three subjectivities in poetry of engagement. Becoming aware of intersections between racial, class, and environmental issues has led to explorations of subjectivity in my own poetry, and I'm interested in how this occurs in some poems I love. In my examples, there is a multiple or polyphonic speaker, a spiritually risky speaker, and a speakerless presentation of other vocabularies. When poets explore subjectivity, it can be instructive for their poems. As I wrote about earth, air, water, fire, and wood, there were secondary brendas and nanobrendas poking through the various stances. There are multiple subjectivities in each of us as we try to express our souls in poems. In this poem from his experimental text *Trilce*, César Vallejo, activist, inventor, interrogator of modernism, uses a polyphonic speakingness in one of the poems.

## Trilce XVIII

Oh, the four walls of the cell!
Ah, the four whitening walls
Which never fail to add up to the same number!

Seedbeds of nerves, evil aperture,
How it snatches from its four corners
At the daily chained extremities!

Kind turnkey of innumerable keys,
If you were here, if you could see
Till what hour these walls remain four
We should both be against them, we two,

More two than ever. And neither should you weep.
Speak, O liberator!

Ah, the walls of the cell!
Meanwhile I am hurt all the more
By the two long ones which, this night, possess
Something of mothers already dead,
Each leading a child by the hand
Down bromine steeps.

And I am left alone,
The right hand upraised, which serves for both,
Seeking the third arm
Which, between my where and my when
Must look for man's powerless superiority.

I admire the multiple forms and stances Vallejo cre-
ates, stretching, breaking open, and twisting vocabu-
lary and grammar to express moral disappointments
and hopes, radically mixing autochthonous languages
with Spanish. Like Celan, like Hopkins, he had to twist
the language, invent neologisms, substitute nouns for
verbs to arrive at his most accurate forms of expression,
which for him were deeply personal as well as political.
*Trilce* was published in 1922 before the Spanish Civil
War. Vallejo was in Paris, questioning the pure aesthet-
icism of modernism. As a Marxist, he was conflicted
about whether art should be pleasurable and deco-

rative, hermetic or public. Unable to resolve this, he places the suffering and confusion in his syntax. In this piece, either remembering the cell walls from his jail time in Peru or describing a hotel room in Paris where he was starving, he addresses aspects of himself and an internalized lover with an inclusive subjectivity that is angular, intimate, and mythic. H. R. Hays's English version keeps this quality in the surreal and gothic phrases: "Seedbeds of nerves, evil aperture" and "daily chained extremities." Many of Vallejo's poems present the poetic self in its paradoxes and tormented dualities—"entre mi dónde y mi cuándo," "between my where and my when"—so the subjective both is and isn't personal.

|   |   |   |   |   \   |   |   |   |   |   )   \   |   |   \   |

Another poem of vital subjectivity is by Solmaz Sharif, an Iranian American poet who writes in "The End of Exile" of returning to Shiraz, Iran.

As the dead, so I come
to the city I am of.
Am without.

To watch play out around me
as theater—

audience as the dead are audience

to the life that is not mine.
Is as not
as never.

Turning down Shiraz's streets
it turns out to be such
a faraway thing.

A without which
I have learned to be.

From bed, I hear a man in the alley
selling something, no longer by mule and holler
but by bullhorn and jalopy.

How to say what he is selling—

it is no thing
this language thought worth naming.
No thing I have used before.

It is his
life I don't see daily.
Not theater. Not play.

Though I remain only audience.

It is a thing he must sell daily
and every day he peddles

this thing: a without which

I cannot name.

Without which is my life.

Sharif narrates with a similar negative capability as Vallejo but in almost diaphanously clear short sentences with a fairly direct syntax. The sentence fragments, short lines, and enjambments of this spare lyric poem allow prepositions both to float and to control the action, especially "to" and "as"; the word *without* appears in the poem four times. "As the dead" is the first of these phrases; her family roots lie in Shiraz, yet this is an experience of alienation and dislocation. The speaker senses a deep connection to the country of her family origin, but remains only "audience" and "no thing"; the poem ends with three substantial lines: "a without which // I cannot name. // Without which is my life." The poet demonstrates fully what it means to be in a place and yet to be conscious of absence; Sharif's negative capability is an active nothing that brings simultaneously a sense of searching bafflement and of openness about the relationship to her family history.

| | | \ | | | \ | | | | | ) \ |

The last poem I will share in this lecture and in my series of lectures is by Forrest Gander, whose poems and translations forge profound relationships between the self, the planet, and language. This is from the title poem of his book *Twice Alive.*

in the presence of water, photobionts go turgid
in hours of dark respiration, a spermatic green-corn smell
takes the shape of a lamellated mushroom
in cavitating symplasts, spores loosen
into the elongation zone on a night of caterwauling loons

so evening finds us at this woods' edge where
at a dead oak's base
shoestring-rot glimmers, its luminescent
rhizomes reflected from the eyes
of a foraging raccoon that doesn't yet sense us

Gander doesn't just pursue the sensuality of the technical vocabulary—"photobiont," "respiration," "lamellated," "symplasts," and "rhizomes"—he also makes organic and inorganic connections to shake up the very idea of the subjective self, one part of which is an onlooker. The poet reaches more deeply into the human order not to center it but to get past the ego to a place where the language and the earth touch and meld with the noticing. Gander and other ecologically committed poets such as Ed Roberson and Brian Teare offer bridges between perception and special vocabularies, suggesting that there is an observing self that is collective and personal, a language for lichen, a raccoon, a drought-driven wildfire that will keep the subject both emotion-driven and lyrical but also dispersed. New subjectivities are needed in the poetry of current environmental concerns. Ecopoetry recalls that humans are not the center but only one of 8.7 million other species. The human gut microbiome is a condominium for at least 300 species of bacteria. I have a great deal of respect for bacteria, especially the kind I mentioned in the refinery action, adapting to their tasks.

Ecological poetry like Forrest Gander's brings together some of the values I've spoken of tonight: emphasis on process, the hope of justice, the decentered self that interrogates otherness. What is your experience, we can ask the hills or bodies of water. What is the experience of shale, not yet mined for its oil? Magical thinking is sometimes a term of contempt in our utilitarian culture, but it might mean using intuitive functions. Our knowledge is deepening.

|   |   |   |   |   \   |   |   |   |   |   |   \   |   )   \   |

I want to close these lectures with hope. I ask that you start envisioning some small actions you can do in addition to your writing. If you're a poet, it is easy to see why you think art is your main task and it is; the values of poetry and art can transform culture, so please tuck this request away for when the vaccinations are further along. Our great sensitivity as poets needn't make us incapable of going outside of our comfort zones; we can hold our government accountable for combating systemic racism, injustice, and planetary endangerment, even though the profit system is entrenched. Some actions involve the patient work of legal processes, or the daily work, as Claudia Rankine suggests, of having difficult conversations. There are eighteen thousand police departments in the United States. After the antiracism protests of last summer, I thought of things I want to do, as an older middle-class white woman in a mixed neighborhood, when it's safe to do so; I want to go talk to my police chief. The thought made me immediately uncomfortable.

What if you are too tired or too stressed? In my childhood, I had the concept of tithing; you give a portion of what you have. Now I tithe my energy, as well as money; I tithe a portion of what I am capable of. If I am low energy this week, my tithe is to write a single letter, but to write by hand, not email, and to use a stamp. If I feel peppy, I can organize something or conceive of an action on Thursday or Friday. Once when I had more zip I took crypto-animist activism to Sacramento; now I'm a tired grandmother and can do less, but not nothing. I want to inspire you not only with poems but by asking that you move what makes you uncomfortable to take part in acts of love and justice. If you are at the Univer-

Ramalina menziesii in west Marin

sity of Virginia, I have an idea for an action we could do together if I visit someday in person.

I want to thank you for your interest in poetry as readers, artists, scientists, and other thinking people; please keep poetry in your lives. Perhaps neither the actions I describe nor poetry itself will change anything but the values they represent will help a lot. I hope in my three talks I've offered some helpful tools on metaphor, metonymy, meaning, mystery, magic, and morality. I could have written hundreds of pages on any of these topics. Thank you so much for your attention over these weeks; I invite you to join me in a life of radical hope, love, and imagination Here's a picture of *Ramalina menziesii*, California state lichen, just because it's strong yet ethereal. And now I'll take a few questions.

# ACKNOWLEDGMENTS

Thank you to all the faculty and staff at the University of Virginia who made my virtual residency possible in 2021; I'd like to thank especially Lisa Russ Spaar and Jeb Livingood for facilitating my talks and class visits; thank you to Rita Dove, Debra Nystrom, Kiki Petrosino, and Brian Teare for inviting me to be the Kapnick Writer. Thank you to the University of Virginia poetry students who brought wonderful poems to office hours online. Thank you to Dr. Dan Kinney for the use of his photo of Tucson and to Angie Hogan, Wren Morgan Myers, and Fernando Campos at and the University of Virginia Press. Thank you to Natalie Dunn for help with permissions, support, and preparation of the manuscript.

Many thanks to family and friends as always for support, especially those who kept us company during the time of this writing. Thank you to Jesse Nathan, and most of all, my husband Bob Hass and to our children and grandchildren, especially to Leon Légère who read poetry with us online throughout the year of lockdown. Love keeps us going.

|   |   |   |   |   \   |   |   |   |   |   )   \   |

All images by Brenda Hillman except as noted: Bob Hass, p. 64; Metropolitan Museum of Art, p. 15; photo by Dr. Taz Kinney, courtesy of Dr. Daniel Kinney, p. 20; Wellcome Collection, p. 66; Wikimedia Commons, CC BY-SA, p. 3 (Materialscientist), p. 9 (VJAnderson), p. 29 (Dori).

|   |   |   |   |   \   |   |   |   |   |   )   \   |

The following poems are used by permission:

Alfred A. Knopf, an imprint of the Knopf Doubleday Publishing Group, a division of Penguin Random House LLC: Wallace Stevens, "The Motive for Metaphor," from The Collected Poems of Wallace Stevens, © 1954, renewed 1982 by Holly Stevens.

Gennady Aygi estate: Gennady Aygi, "Field: In the Full Blaze of Winter," translated by Peter France.

Counterpoint Press: Tomas Tranströmer, "Below Freezing," translated by Robert Bly.

Ben Friedlander: Paul Celan, "[Eternity decays: in]," translated by Ben Friedlander.

Harper Collins: Robert Hass, "To a Reader," © 1979.

New Directions Publishing Corp: Robert Duncan, "Often I Am Permitted to Return to a Meadow," from The Opening of the Field, © 1960; Forest Gander, "Twice Alive" from Twice Alive, © 2019, 2020, 2021; Kim Hyesoon, "Already: Day Twenty-Eight," from Autobiography of Death, translated from the Korean by Don Mee Choi, © 2016.

The Permissions Company, LLC: Tongo Eisen-Martin, "Heaven Is All Goodbyes," from Heaven Is All Goodbyes, © 2017, City Lights Books; Harryette Mullen, "[why these blues come from us]," from Recyclopedia, © 2006, Graywolf Press; Solmaz Sharif, "The End of Exile," from Customs, © 2018, 2022, Graywolf Press; Layli Long Soldier, "[Whereas at four years old I read the first chapter of the Bible aloud I was not Christian]," from Whereas, © 2017 Graywolf Press; Arthur Sze, excerpt from "Sight Lines," from Sight Lines, © 2019, Copper Canyon Press; Simone White, "[There was a time I hardly went three steps]," from Of Being Dispersed, © 2016, Futurepoem Books; C. D. Wright, "Poem Missing Someone," from ShallCross, © 2016, Copper Canyon Press.

Princeton University Press: Yannis Ritsos, "Miniature," translated by Edmund "Mike" Keely.

Wesleyan University Press: Camille Dungy, "Brevity," from Trophic Cascade, © 2017; Evie Shockley, "my last modernist poem #4 (or re re-birth of a nation)," from the new black, ©2011.